P9-DGB-294

"*I'd Rather Be Reading* is a book lover's delight. Readers will be reminded of the books that shaped their own lives (and maybe add a few more to the list)."

Annie Spence, librarian and author of *Dear Fahrenheit 451: Love and Heartbreak in the Stacks*

"Anne Bogel's beguiling latest is a love letter to the reading life, infused with all the warmth, charm, and brilliance her fans have come to expect. I found myself—and my reading community—inside its pages, and you will too."

Joshilyn Jackson, *New York Times* bestselling author of *The Almost Sisters*

"Personal and fun, Anne Bogel's essay collection is a self-portrait in books—weaving together all the readers she has been. *I'd Rather Be Reading* is her winsome musings on books, not just as a way to enjoy a good story, but as a way to become a whole person. Anne believes books find their way to you when you need them. You need this book in your reading life."

Kathleen Grissom, author of *The Kitchen House*

"This book is a reader's delight. Lovely illustrations and Anne's witty commentary will keep you laughing and nodding all the way through. Whether you gulp it down or revisit it time and time again, *I'd Rather Be Reading* will make you crazy grateful for your own unique reading life."

Sarah Mackenzie, author of *The Read-Aloud Family* and host of the *Read-Aloud Revival* podcast

"Books help make us who we are, and they make us better people. Anne Bogel's charming essays in *I'd Rather Be Reading*, all about the bibliophile's journey through life, will make you fall in love with books all over again."

Jane Mount, founder of Ideal Bookshelf and author of *Bibliophile: An Illustrated Miscellany for People Who Love Books*

"In this thoughtful essay collection, Anne Bogel reminds even the most weary reader among us that there is no greater pastime than that of getting lost in a good book. *I'd Rather Be Reading* is a charming exploration of all the ways books entertain, challenge, and change us. It's a call to read with exuberant joy and a meditation on the things that hinder us from doing so. A must-read for anyone who calls themselves a book lover!"

Ariel Lawhon, author of *I Was Anastasia*

I'd Rather Be
READING

I'd Rather Be READING

THE DELIGHTS AND DILEMMAS

OF THE READING LIFE

ANNE BOGEL

BakerBooks

a division of Baker Publishing Group
Grand Rapids, Michigan

Published by Baker Books
a division of Baker Publishing Group
PO Box 6287, Grand Rapids, MI 49516-6287
www.bakerbooks.com

Printed in the United States of America

Library of Congress Cataloging-in-Publication Data
Names: Bogel, Anne, 1978– author.
Title: I'd rather be reading : the delights and dilemmas of the reading life
    / Anne Bogel.
Other titles: I would rather be reading
Description: Grand Rapids : Baker Publishing Group, 2018. | Includes
    bibliographical references.
Identifiers: LCCN 2018007036 | ISBN 9780801072925 (cloth)
Subjects: LCSH: Books and reading.
Classification: LCC Z1003 .B685 2018 | DDC 028/.9—dc23
LC record available at https://lccn.loc.gov/2018007036

Cover and interior artwork: David Holmes 2018

The author is represented by the William K Jensen Literary Agency.

18   19   20   21   22   23   24   7   6   5   4   3

For everyone who's ever finished a book
under the covers with a flashlight
when they were supposed to be sleeping.

Ah, how good it is to be among people who are reading!

—Rainer Maria Rilke

Books wrote our life story, and as they accumulated on our shelves (and on our windowsills, and underneath our sofa, and on top of our refrigerator), they became chapters in it themselves. How could it be otherwise?

—Anne Fadiman

Contents

Contents

Introduction

The Pages of Our Lives

Can you recommend a great book?"

Because I'm a writer, certified book nerd, and all-around bookish enthusiast, people ask me this question all the time. I talk about books like it's my job—and in a sense, it is. I make book recommendations every day.

When a reader tells me they're looking for a great book to read, it doesn't seem like a complicated question, or like they're asking for too much. I can imagine where they're coming from because I've been there myself. Maybe they've read through a string of mediocre titles, or maybe it's been a while since they've read anything at all. Maybe they're in a slump, reading-wise, and it's killed the confidence they once had in choosing good titles for themselves. They're not in the mood to take a chance; they're looking for a sure thing—a book they're guaranteed to love.

But no library or bookstore has a dedicated shelf for "great books," at least not the kind we're talking about here. Maybe they have a section of impressive-looking hardbacks, those hundred or so titles some consider to be the foundation of Western literature—Plato, Cicero, Dante. Those Great Books are easy enough to find, but they're not what you're looking for when you want a great book.

You're looking for a book that reminds you why you read in the first place. One written well and that will feel like it was written just for you—one that will make you think about things in a new way, or feel things you didn't expect a book to make you feel, or see things in a new light. A book you won't want to put down, whose characters you don't want to tell good-bye. A book you will close feeling satisfied and grateful, thinking, *Now, that was a good one.*

If I could read only great books for the rest of my days, I would be happy. But finding those books—for myself or any other reader—isn't so easy. A "great" book means different things to different people.

When we talk about reading, we often focus on the books themselves, but so much of the reading life is about the reader as an active participant. To put a great book in your hands, here's what I need to know: When you turn to the written word, what are you looking for? What themes speak to you? What sorts of places do you want to vicariously visit? What types of characters do you enjoy meeting on the page? What was the last story you wished would never end? Which was the last volume you hurled across the room?

Without the details of what "great" means to you, and without knowing what kind of reader you are, the question might be simple, but it's impossible to answer. To hand you a great book, I don't just need to know about books; I need to know *you*.

A book is just printed words on a page: you can shelve it, shred it, ship it around the world. It's a commodity you can buy and sell, highly prize, or box up in your basement and leave to mildew. We both loan them and discard them.

But avid readers know a great book doesn't exist only in the realm of the material. The words between those covers bring whole worlds to life. When I think of the characters and stories and ideas contained on a single shelf of my personal library, it boggles my mind. To readers, those books—the ones we buy and borrow and trade and sell—are more than objects. They are opportunities beckoning us. When we read, we connect with them (or don't) in a personal way.

Sometimes the personal nature of reading is kind of a pain, making it difficult to find a great book for an individual reader. Sometimes finding the right book feels like a hassle—especially if you're standing in the bookstore aisle or perusing the library stacks or even scrutinizing the teetering pile on your nightstand, debating what to read next—when all you want to do is find a book you will love, that you'll close in the span of a few hours or days or weeks and say, "That was *amazing*." A great book. That's all you want. But reading is personal. We can't know what a book will mean to us until we read it. And so we take a leap and choose.

Sometimes we'll choose a book that's all wrong for us; that's a peril of the reading life. Sometimes we'll read through a string of mediocre titles, or we'll find ourselves in a slump. Sometimes we'll read a perfectly good book, but the timing's all wrong; the same book means different things to different people, or in different seasons of life. Since reading is personal, it can be tricky. (Not such a commodity after all, eh?)

We are readers. Books are an essential part of our lives and of our life stories. For us, reading isn't just a hobby or a pastime; it's a lifestyle. We're the kind of people who understand the heartbreak of not having your library reserves come in before you leave town for vacation and the exhilaration of stumbling upon the new Louise Penny at your local independent bookstore three whole days before the official publication date. We know the pain of investing hours of reading time in a book we enjoyed right up until the final chapter's truly terrible resolution, and we know the pleasure of stumbling upon exactly the right book at exactly the right time.

There are few one-size-fits-all prescriptions for the reading life. This spurs all sorts of readerly dilemmas, but it also brings readers endless delight.

In this book, we'll dive into the personal nature of reading—what shapes us as readers, what we bring to the page. We'll explore how to read, how to choose good books, and what happens when we read bad ones. We'll dive into why we connect with some books so powerfully. We'll peek into other people's reading lives. And we'll enjoy every minute of it, because that's the kind of people we are.

How good it is to be among people who are reading.

1

Confess Your Literary Sins

In David Lodge's campus novel *Changing Places*, two college professors—one American, one British—swap teaching roles for a year. In one memorable scene, the British academics invite their American guest to play a party game called Humiliation. Players confess important literary works they haven't yet read, and points are scored based on how many other players have already read them. The person with the most—and most egregious—gaps in their personal reading history wins. If everyone but you has read that book, you're going to be great at Humiliation.

Those fictional professors aren't the only ones who enjoy shocking and delighting their fellow readers by spilling the guilty secrets of their reading lives, sharing those works they suspect everyone but them has already read, or perhaps the books they love but feel they shouldn't. Why can we not help but laugh when we discover an English prof has never read *Hamlet* (as in *Changing Places*), or that a serious friend has a thing for Sophie Kinsella novels, or that a soft-spoken friend is obsessed with celebrity memoirs, or our friend with the religion PhD has never read C. S. Lewis?

Why do these revelations delight us so? Screenwriters have a name for it. They call it the comedy gap, that gap between what we *expect* to happen and what *actually* happens. Or, in this case, what we *expect* a person's reading life to be like and what it's *truly* like.

In 2011, I named my new blog *Modern Mrs Darcy*, because it captured the timeless and timely nature of what I wanted to write about—and because I love Jane Austen.* Almost exactly five years later, in 2016, I started a podcast called *What Should I Read Next?* devoted to book talk, reading recommendations, and literary matchmaking. The funny thing about creating a blog using a name from a Jane Austen novel, or casting yourself as a literary matchmaker, is how many readers you meet feel as though a conversation with you is an invitation to play Humiliation.

*Emma and *Persuasion* are my *other* very favorite Jane Austen novels, but *Modern Mrs Knightley* didn't have the same ring, and Anne Elliot and I share a first name, which seemed confusing.

Since I began these projects, I've been surprised to find myself a magnet for readers' literary confessions: so many readers feel compelled to confess important literary works they haven't yet read, or that they love the "wrong" books, or that they don't read much at all lately.

These readers are acutely aware of their own gap: that divide between what they *think* their reading life should be like and what it's *really* like.

Sometimes I think they're sharing in fun. They're content with their choices and opinions, but they appreciate the pleasure of divulging guilty secrets and see in me a kindred spirit, one who will appreciate their confession. But the truths of many readers' reading lives make them uncomfortable; their gap isn't a source of amusement, but frustration. They're certain their taste is questionable, their opinions are wrong, their reading habits are poor, and it's only a matter of time before the Book Police track them down. They're carrying guilty reading secrets that make them feel as though they aren't *real* readers. They're partly terrified of being found out and partly feel they might burst if they can't tell *someone* their bookish secrets.

Often that someone is me: these readers find me—in person or online—and say, "I don't usually tell people this . . ." before spilling their secrets:

They've never read Shakespeare or Chaucer, Brontë or Austen, Hawthorne or Dickens, or any other author you might possibly have been assigned in high school.

They *were* assigned these books in school, but never read them.

They wrote their term papers on Important Novels without reading the important novels. (The better their grade, the worse they feel.)

They've never read Jane Austen. Specifically, they've never read *Pride and Prejudice*. They once read Jane Austen, but they don't understand the fuss. They attempted Jane Austen but couldn't get past the first chapter. They read *Pride and Prejudice*, but they liked the movie better—and not even the one with Colin Firth, which they think I could understand, but the other one. The crown of their home library is a beautiful Jane Austen box set—and they *still* haven't read Jane Austen.

They're an English Lit major who did all the required reading—and hated a healthy percentage of it. They think *Moby-Dick* is trash. Also, *The Sound and the Fury*. And everything by James Joyce.

They don't understand the love for *To Kill a Mockingbird*, *East of Eden*, *The Great Gatsby*, and any number of beloved American classics. They just don't care. ("Can you say *boring*?")

They hate *Charlotte's Web*, *The Wind in the Willows*, *The Giving Tree*.

They hate the Twilight series so much they want to flip over bookstore displays.

They finally succumbed to the hype and read the Harry Potter series, and they think it's drivel.

I BOTH wished   which fol-
lowed this sleepless night: I wanted to hear his voice again, yet feared
to meet his eye. During the early part of the morning I momentarily
expected his coming; he was not in the frequent habit of entering the
schoolroom; but he did step in for a few minutes sometimes, and I had
the impression that he was sure to visit it that day.

They teach ninth-grade English by day and currently binge on the Twilight series at night, for the sixth time in as many years. ("Please don't tell my students.")

They don't understand how anyone could not love *The Catcher in the Rye*. They are obsessed with Holden Caulfield. They wonder what this says about them. They are not adolescent males, so they're pretty sure it's not good.

They're obsessed with the Harry Potter books.

They've read the Outlander series eight times. They're counting down to the next installment the way they once counted down to their wedding day or the birth of a child. They wrote Diana Gabaldon a fan letter, begging her to write faster.

They own forty-two cozy mysteries, whose covers all feature a skein of yarn, a pie, or both.

They are addicted to firehouse romances, the kind whose covers bear rippled torsos, and they don't even bother to buy the more sedate-looking Kindle versions anymore, because the e-reader experience just isn't the same.

They tried to read the latest thought-provoking National Book Award winner on the beach but couldn't get into it. So they made an emergency vacation bookstore run for a stack of baby-blue books by Elin Hilderbrand, Mary Kay Andrews, and Dorothea Benton Frank, whose covers all bore sandy beach scenes, all of which were inhaled that week. (They still haven't read the award winner.)

They haven't read much of anything lately, unless their iPad counts. Or *In Style* magazine. Or the tabloid covers in the grocery checkout line.

They've had the same book sitting on their nightstand for three years and haven't opened it once.

They've never, not ever, read a book over three hundred pages long.

They've tried and tried, but they haven't enjoyed a book written by a woman in years. Or a man. Or a white person. Or someone who doesn't live in England or the United States. Or Alaska. Or the American South.

They checked a book out of the library four years ago—and still haven't returned it. They're afraid to show their face at the library until they pay down their overdue balance, which now equals the cost of a nice dinner out. The library canceled their card because of lost books and overdue fines.

They ordered pizza so they could skip making dinner and finish their book. They ate cereal for dinner so they could finish their book. They forgot to eat dinner because they were finishing their book.

The last time they finished a great story, the book hangover lasted three days. They were so caught up in their book that they let the kids draw on the walls so they could get to the last page. They locked themselves in the bathroom so they could read undisturbed.

They think they might love books too much.

Whatever it may be, they're sure they're the only one with this issue.

Reader, whatever secret you're keeping, it's time to spill it. I'll take your confession, but the absolution is unnecessary. These secrets aren't sins; they're just secrets. No need to repent. C. S. Lewis once wrote, "Friendship . . . is born at the moment when one man says to another, 'What! You too? I thought I was the only one.'"

Reader, you're not the only one. Keep confessing to your fellow readers; tell them what your reading life is *really* like. They'll understand. They may even say, "You too?" And when they do, you've found a friend. And the beginnings of a great book club.

2

The Books That Find You

Sarah Addison Allen's charming debut novel, *Garden Spells*, features a character who feels compelled to give odd little gifts to her friends and neighbors: strawberry Pop-Tarts, two quarters, a silk shirt that's three sizes too big. There's a bit of magic about each gift, because the giver never knows what it's for when she gives it. Yet the gift always turns out to be vital to the recipient, who soon finds she needs strawberry Pop-Tarts for an unexpected guest, or two quarters to make an emergency phone call, or whose life changes when she goes to exchange the shirt. Each gift seems odd—even random—when it's given, but it turns out to be exactly what the recipient needs, at exactly the right time.*

---

*Allen's books often have a bit of magic about them. In *The Sugar Queen*, one woman's unique gift is that the specific book she needs in

I've been fortunate to receive quite a few of these magical gifts. Not in the form of breakfast treats, or coins, or clothing, but time after time I've been given a strange, unexpected, and completely perfect gift: a book. Not any book, but the *right* book, right when I needed it.

I choose what to read based on a whim and friends' recommendations, by publication date and library due date. I don't carefully plan exactly what I'm going to read next, and in what order. I may walk into a bookstore and leave with my next read at the emphatic urging of an excited bookseller, even if I didn't know that book existed an hour before. Maybe three unrelated people recommend the same book to me in the course of a week, and I decide to take the hint. Maybe my kids tell me I *have* to read a certain title, or for reasons I can't articulate, I decide it's finally time to pull one of those unread paperbacks off my own shelves and get to reading.

I don't carefully plan—and yet it's uncanny how often I seem to be reading just the right book at just the right time. Sometimes I feel compelled to read a book—or someone feels compelled to recommend it—for reasons I can't discern, and only later do I find it's essential to me, right then. Not before I started reading it, but after. The book

---

her life right then mysteriously appears—on her bedside table, on her desk at work, in her handbag. Because of the nature of its contents, she knows exactly why it's there—unlike the strawberry Pop-Tarts.

may seem random when I choose it, but halfway through I realize, *I need this right now.*

Call it chance, or fate, or divine providence. Blame it on probabilities or my own state of mind—when the student is ready, the teacher appears, etcetera. Credit it to dumb luck. I just know it's served me well to pay attention to subtle hints, and that includes hints about books.

A decade ago, it seemed like everyone I knew was telling me to read Dallas Willard's *The Divine Conspiracy.* So when I saw the five-dollar hardcover on the remainder table at our now-defunct local bookstore, I snatched it up—and didn't read it. Years later, someone or something inspired me to pick it up again. I began reading, a few pages at a time, finding it wasn't the kind of book I could read quickly. I was a few chapters in when my son was unexpectedly diagnosed with something scary, out of the clear blue sky. He was fine, and then he wasn't—and it happened fast. He was diagnosed just before lunch, and by dinnertime we were on a plane to visit a world-class medical specialist. (Pro tip: when only the best will do, you're in trouble.)

We packed in a mad rush, tossing essentials into our suitcases, including our current reads. (I never leave home without a book, even in an emergency.) Had I been in the middle of a legal thriller, or fluffy romance, or parenting book, I would have grabbed that. But *The Divine*

Conspiracy was the book on my nightstand, so that book—about living right, and living well, and beginning to do so *right now*—accompanied me to unfamiliar doctors' offices, airplane terminals, hotel rooms, waiting rooms, recovery wings. Willard seemed to be speaking only to me, telling me exactly what I needed to hear, moments before I needed to hear it. He told me how to hang in there and how to hang on, how to get my head straight and my heart settled. I couldn't have asked for a better companion for that journey.

If this has happened to you—if the right book has almost magically appeared in your life at the right time to hold your hand for the journey—you know it feels like a special kind of grace.

A few summers ago Parker J. Palmer's *Let Your Life Speak* was the book I couldn't escape. I owned a copy, and I had been meaning to read it for years, but I kept putting it off. The book, published in 2000, wasn't old, but it wasn't exactly hot off the press. So when numerous friends and acquaintances happened to bring it up over a week or two, speaking of its importance in their lives, asking if I'd read it yet, I paid attention. I took the hint.

I moved *Let Your Life Speak* from my bookshelf to my nightstand. In it, Palmer wrestles with vocation and calling and making tough decisions in these areas. These were topics I'd been wrestling through, although my fellow readers didn't know that. It was the book I needed, right then.

Why this book, or that one? I never know at the time. Sometimes, of course, I seek out a book I need. But sometimes it's more apt to say the book seeks me. I've learned books move in mysterious ways, and I'd do well to pay attention.

Sometimes these serendipitous reads are of big-picture, soul-level importance, like Willard and Palmer were to me. But sometimes they're right in more prosaic ways—a book that makes you laugh when you desperately need comic relief, or provides needed practical advice about a subject you're struggling with, or delivers important information just before you need it.

Last year I happened to read Chris Voss's *Never Split the Difference* while we were negotiating the sale of our old house. The author, a former FBI hostage negotiator, recounts fascinating tales from his days at the bureau. His specialty was international kidnapping negotiations, and those stories didn't unfold like I anticipated. (It turns out what I expected kidnappers want from a negotiation and what they actually want are very different things.) I was impressed by how Voss applied the principles he developed from high-stakes talks with hostage-takers to comparatively mundane acts like negotiating a salary, or talking with your teenager about her day, or buying a house. Or, more aptly, selling a house.

I read the book in only two days, passed it to my husband, who did the same, and then—with our Realtor's encouragement—we put Voss's advice into action. We established a high anchor price and didn't leave much room to negotiate. We phrased our starting and counteroffers carefully, relying on his guidelines. We sold our house on the first day, for more than the asking price. Right book, right time.

Years ago I happened to read *The Geography of Nowhere*, with its dedicated chapter on Seaside, Florida, just weeks before a long-planned trip to the region. We drove twenty minutes out of our way and experienced the small city that sounded so interesting on the page. I read the fascinating Frederick Law Olmsted biography *A Clearing in the Distance* just before a visit to Chicago, where I visited the Olmsted-designed parks and neighborhoods I'd just read about. I happened to read *Walkable City*, with its copious Manhattan examples, right before a trip to New York City, and the timing made my Manhattan experience infinitely richer.

Once, I finished a nonfiction book about urban parks and then showed up at a cocktail party, now knowledgeable about the one thing I didn't know a rarely seen distant relative loved to talk about. Instead of chatting about the weather or how long it had been since we'd seen each other, we had a delightful conversation about the history of landscape architecture. Word got back to me later that she was newly hopeful about the younger generations because I spoke intelligently about a subject dear to her heart. (Thank goodness I happened to read that book when I did.)

As a devoted reader, I lovingly give countless hours to finding the right books for me. I don't think those hours are wasted; part of the fun of reading is *planning* the reading. But I've learned that sometimes, despite my best efforts, a book unexpectedly finds me and not the other way around. And when it does, it's okay to reshuffle my To Be Read list and go with it.

3

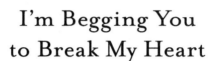

I'm Begging You
to Break My Heart

I can still picture the scene. A late fall afternoon, south-ern light slanting through the tall windows onto the wooden desks of our fifth-grade classroom, our teacher sitting primly in her straight-backed chair, legs crossed at the ankles, a worn copy of *Where the Red Fern Grows* in her hands. Not one of us knew what we were in for.

She'd taught fifth grade for twenty-five years. I don't remember a warning, but surely she knew what was about to happen. By the time she read the last page, there wasn't a dry eye in the classroom. Girls sobbed, some of us to the point that we couldn't catch our breath. Others sat with tears quietly trickling down their faces. At the sink,

I grabbed crunchy brown paper towels to wipe my eyes. A friend joined me, hand proffered, and I gave him one.

"Thanks," he said. "It's not the book or anything. My allergies are really bad this year."

Sure they are, John.

By age ten, I'd already read hundreds, if not thousands, of books. But that was the first time a book provoked a visceral, gut-wrenching, puddle-of-tears reaction. Before that day, I didn't know a book could do that to a person. I didn't know I could care so much about events that happened on the page. I didn't know an author could convince me—if only for a moment—that what happened there was real.

The best books move you, drawing out the full range of emotions from the reader, and sometimes that includes breaking your heart. Not every reader enjoys this experience. (Some adult readers claim they were scarred for life by their own grade-school experience reading tearful classics like *Where the Red Fern Grows, Old Yeller,* or *Bridge to Terabithia.*) But we still admire—albeit sometimes grudgingly— what an author accomplishes when he or she makes us cry.

Sometimes you know the tears are coming. The sad parts aren't going to blindside you; you know going in to expect a tearjerker. *The Fault in Our Stars, Me Before You,* and—unless you're an innocent fifth grader who doesn't yet know the scoop—*Where the Red Fern Grows.* You pick up these notoriously gut-wrenching titles only if you're

not opposed to a good cry; maybe you even welcome one. (These are such reliable heartbreakers that if you don't cry, you might worry about yourself: *Do I really have a heart?*)

Sometimes a moment resonates specifically with *you*, personally, in a way that wouldn't send another reader running for the Kleenex, because it touches on something you've experienced in your own life. When our twelve-year-old chocolate lab died, I found a copy of *Dog Heaven*, gathered all the kids on the couch, and we cried our way through it together. The book spoke to where we were, capturing the truth of our experience, validating our loss.

Sometimes the tears surprise you. I finished listening to *A Man Called Ove* on audio while getting ready for church on a Sunday morning. I had so little idea what was coming that I swiped on mascara while listening to the book's final minutes, unafraid. But Fredrik Backman made me laugh, and then sob, almost simultaneously, with the inky wand still in hand. I had to wash my product-streaked, tear-stained face and start over. (We were late for church that day.)

Sometimes a great book makes us feel the loss of what could have been—a dream, a baby, a future. Several years ago I read Doris Kearns Goodwin's excellent Abraham Lincoln biography *Team of Rivals*. I knew the basic outline of his life from history class; American students know that story's sad ending. But Goodwin's version astonished me, making me feel, for the first time, an overwhelming sense of how much was lost that night at Ford's Theatre—by his family, yes, but also by the nation and the world.

Goodwin demonstrates how important Lincoln was to the cause of what was right, painting a vivid picture of what he accomplished in office, of what he was carefully working toward after the Civil War, and of why the man himself was desperately needed. And then they killed him. When she described what happened that awful night in Ford's Theatre and across the city, I felt like I was there, and for the first time I understood the scope of the disaster and how it affects me even now. I didn't expect her history to make me weep, but it did—because Goodwin made me feel its weight.

Sometimes a book prods you to grieve with its characters. You're immersed in the story, so much so that you feel what they're feeling. When a beloved character experiences loss—of someone they love, of a friendship, of their innocence—you feel their pain. When he grieves, you grieve with him. Sometimes you grieve the characters themselves: they die, you feel like you've lost a friend, and you weep.

Sometimes a book brings the tears because you don't want it to end. You've been on a journey together, you and your fictional friends, and you don't want to close that literal chapter of your life and move on. When my daughter read Holly Goldberg Sloan's novel *Short*, she cried so hard she scared me a little. The novel is about an unlikely band of people who experience something exceptional together, and when their time together ends, the book ends too. When I asked if they were happy tears or sad tears, she told me through sobs that they were good tears: she was *just so sorry it was over*.

I don't relish crying over a book, but I'll say this: it's not easy to earn a reader's tears—and if an author writes well enough to earn mine, I'm in.

Pass the tissues. It's time to read.

4

The Books Next Door

A single conversation in 1999 changed my life, although I didn't know it at the time. I wasn't even present. My mom was visiting an old friend, thirty years her senior, and as women often do, they talked about their children. My mom told her friend that my longtime boyfriend, Will, had just popped the question. We'd be getting married in a year, after we graduated from college, and we hoped we could afford a little starter house in town.

"Maybe they'd be interested in mine," this woman said.

The house wasn't actually hers, but she'd been tasked with selling it on behalf of a friend's estate. The woman had been a spunky widow much loved by her friends and neighbors, and her last significant purchase had been a red sports car. She had died a few years earlier at age ninety-three, leaving behind her 1939 Cape Cod, which she purchased new that year for two hundred dollars.

We went to check it out. The house was neglected: white paint peeling on the outside, mint-green paint peeling on the inside, floors covered in faded linoleum and torn green shag. The air-conditioning hadn't worked in years, and the electrician stamped dire warnings on our inspection. But the house had good vibes and good bones, the price was right, and it was next door to the library.

It was perfect.

When we moved in, three weeks shy of my twenty-second birthday, I wasn't yet the reader I would become. I loved to read, but I wasn't yet—how should I put it?—a true bibliophile. (Although now I wonder if *addict* better captures the idea.)

The library's proximity was a nice bonus. I'd always used the library. I'd even visited this particular branch as a child. It wasn't a historic library, or a beautiful one, but it had a nice selection, friendly librarians, and convenient hours. And it was *mine*.

I had been looking forward to living in our new neighborhood, but before we moved in, I didn't realize just how wonderful it would be. It wasn't until many years later that I appreciated what a special place we'd stumbled upon. I didn't perceive, until years later when we moved away, how the nearness of the library shaped the rhythms of our lives.

I quickly learned it was easy to pop next door. Since the library was so close, I started using it more. I was young and poor, and books occupied a tiny sliver of my careful monthly budget. But the request system could deliver any book in my city's collection to within a hundred yards of my front door with just a few keystrokes, for free—and with a smile and hello when I picked it up. If I needed a new book to read, no problem. There were fifty thousand books next door. My reading life was soon full of instant gratification.

Things shifted abruptly when our first child was born. Desperate for adult interaction and still carrying an extra twenty pounds, I walked to the library every day of my

postpartum recovery. In the early days, the library was a manageable distance to walk to stretch my out-of-shape legs. But then it became my destination for a quick trip to get away by myself when the opportunity arose, if only for five minutes. It was no big deal to run next door, so I did—sometimes multiple times a day.

As my kids grew, the library became part of their daily lives as well. We were there so often the librarians joked about making me a name tag. We never missed a special event or a story time. The kids were young; I didn't mind if they ran inside wearing only bathing suits and cover-ups. We went through a long stage when my toddler refused to wear pants, and so he went to the library without pants. I never would have let him get in the car with no pants on, but the library was just next door. We were barely out of our driveway (I told myself). No big deal.

As a family with young children, sometimes we just needed to get out of the house, even in the rain or rare deep snow. The library was our obvious destination. There was always (and I mean *always*) a reason to go there. Maybe to pick up a reserve item that had come in or drop off a book we'd finished. (We ran out of shelf space fast in a small house with multiple readers.) Decluttering didn't feel complete without a trip next door to complete the cycle, donating our already-read magazines to the community basket or dropping off unwanted books for the sale table.

We knew all the employees, and they knew us. We saw them all the time, as they were taking breaks on the library path by our driveway, practicing yoga in the shady grass, or eating lunch at the outdoor picnic table—the one closer to my kitchen sink than to the library's circulation desk. Some days I saw the circulation workers more than I saw my husband.

We stayed in that tiny starter house much longer than we'd originally intended because we didn't want to leave. Not long after we moved away, my grade-school daughter crafted a wistful essay for school about her first home, with its unique location and shaded yard and flowering trees and nearby walking path. "It sounds like heaven," her teacher commented at our first parent-teacher conference. "Why would you ever move?"

Library or not, we had to deal with reality. Practicalities won out. "One bathroom," we told him.

A parent himself, he understood.

A few years ago, after thirteen years in our first house, we said good-bye to the library next door. We've moved now into an old home I can see being our "forever house," despite the obvious drawback: I can no longer see the library from my kitchen window. But because we hope to spend many years here, the first project we took on after moving was building lots of bookshelves so we'd feel at home—even if we must fill those shelves ourselves.

41

From our new place, it's an easy walk to the closest library, the one we've now made ours. It's a beautiful old Carnegie with a decent selection, friendly staff, and charming little garden. If it hadn't been for that first house, I would feel pampered, library-wise. But there's a difference between visiting the library two or three times a week and two or three times a day, between having a library in your neighborhood and a library in your own backyard. The first is wonderful, but the second is a book lover's dream come true. It was *my* dream come true.

That little house next door to the library is where I grew up as a reader, where I came into my own as one. I read literally thousands of books there. When it comes to all the pages I've read in my life so far, I'm certain I read more pages in that house—in every room, on the patio, while tending the grill, on the front steps while the kids rode their bikes on the sidewalk, and in the hammock under the dogwoods—than I have at any other location on earth, there in the shadow of the library.

Maybe we all look back wistfully at the conversations that changed our fate and the places that shaped us. I was shaped, as a woman and a reader, by a chance conversation between two women, and the first house it brought us, the one next door to the library.

5

Hooked on the Story

As a kid, reading came easily to me, and so I read—blowing through early reader books and chapter books, choose-your-own adventures, time travel novels, popular tween series. Reading was my fun, adult-approved escape, both adventure and leisure.

Somehow—I wish I could remember how—I found my way to the L. M. Montgomery story *Emily of New Moon*, the darker and broodier literary cousin to Montgomery's better-known *Anne* books. Pre-*Emily*, I liked to read—I might even say I *loved* it—but it didn't captivate me. Yet.

Then came *Emily*, the first book I finished under the covers with a flashlight at 2:00 a.m. because I couldn't put it down. The book had a hold on me and wouldn't let go. I was so caught up in Emily's fate I couldn't sleep until I found out *what happened next*. For the first time, I was hooked on the story.

My husband's experience was different, though not uncommon. He was sixteen. He *liked* to read, but he didn't *love* it. Then he picked up *The Firm*, and for the first time he got it. He couldn't sleep until he found out *what happened next*. That experience made him understand what a good book could do, why some people *love* to read. He was hooked.

Now that my own children are getting older, I hope to see them hooked by a good book, by turns. My kids have been reading for years, of course, but they're still learning to appreciate the pleasure and power of a good story.

I think they're getting somewhere. Last summer my teen read the Agatha Christie classic *And Then There Were None*. It was assigned reading for school, not the typical starting point for inviting a kid to fall in love with reading. He began reading, skeptically, but then—as sometimes happens with a good book—the story sucked him in. He kept reading, much faster than required, because he had to figure out the mystery, puzzle over the epilogue's explanation of the perfect crime, and then read it again. He had to know *what happened next*, and he couldn't put the book down until he did. He called it the best book he'd ever read. In hindsight, will he name this as the book that hooked him? I hope so.

Can every devoted reader point back to the book that hooked them on the story? I'd like to think so. Not a book they appreciate, or grudgingly respect, but the one that captivated them, the one they didn't want to put down, the one that made them decide, for themselves, to make reading a part of their life, forever.

6

My Inner Circle

S ome of my best ideas are born of envy. Not the green-
with-it sort, but that brand with which many readers are familiar: book envy. Or more specifically in this
instance, bookshelf envy.

While traveling, we once stayed in the apartment of an
author friend, a little-used second home furnished just
enough to feel homelike. Her full-time residence is pre-
dictably packed with books, but this apartment held only
a few modest bookshelves. One held her current reads,
another her lifetime favorite titles, but one shelf held a
motley assortment of books I couldn't figure out. In addition to her usual jumble of literary fiction, mysteries,
and classics, this shelf held her lesser-read genres—poetry

and science fiction, memoir and self-help—as well as trail guides, neighborhood histories, and recipe collections from small Illinois towns. I couldn't decode the pattern, and I was left in suspense until the author herself provided the key: she calls it her friends and family shelf.

This shelf initially held only books written by true friends, the dozen or two fellow authors she personally knew, and knew well. Because *friends and family* sounded much nicer to her ear, she tacked on the *family*—and reassured herself that some of her friends were dear enough to feel like kin. Since then, her son has written a slim volume of poetry that now graces her shelf, making the moniker both emotionally and technically accurate.

That good idea was begging to be stolen, and I lost no time in doing so, reorganizing my bookshelves (again), emptying a shelf for the purpose of filling it up again with books by friends and wish-they-were family. Not knowing as many authors as my friend, I was forced to be more generous with my definition. I waver on the exact standards: Did someone I meet once at a conference count, or perhaps at a bookstore signing, or that I met in the bathroom at a publishing conference, or exchanged an email with once or twice? (The answer to all these, at one time or another, has been *yes*.)

My shelf holds books by people I know from Twitter, or whom I've met a few times in person, having shared

dinner or drinks once upon a time. It holds books by *actual* friends, and those numbers—of books and of friends—increase every year. I've shelved books by old friends who became authors and by newer friends I met *because* they write books. The shelf holds books by people I talk to on the phone and text when I think a deadline might kill me, friends whose funerals I would hop on a plane to attend should it come to pass that they *are* killed by one of their own dreaded deadlines. It holds books by friends who've seen my home in all its dirty-dishes, cluttered-counters glory, and in whose homes I've seen the same, and by those whose children I know and who know mine.

Then the shelf holds books by those authors with whom I would very much like to be friends, writers whose works have shaped me—who, it seems, *get* me, but will never sit at my table or scratch my dog's ears or use my dirty bathroom. They feel like kindred spirits despite the fact that I've never met them—and never will outside the pages of their work because they lived a hundred years ago.

48

(I'd like to put Jane Austen on this shelf, but I can't bring myself to do it. Instead she remains safely ensconced with my favorites, keeping company with Wendell Berry and Marilynne Robinson and Wallace Stegner—authors with whom I feel compelled to be on my best behavior, who intimidate me too much to feel like friends.)

Some authors I shelve here because we're on a first-name basis, though they would be surprised at this intimacy. I've called Witold Rybczynski by his first name for years simply because I fear I'd butcher the pronunciation of his last name. Dallas Willard is *Dallas* to me—not because Willard isn't easy enough to pronounce, but after talking about him so often, for so long, it seemed silly to keep calling him by his full name, and *Willard* didn't feel right. Madeleine L'Engle is *Madeleine* to me, because I feel like we understand each other. I refer to these authors personally and often, and putting them on the friends and family shelf seems fair, even if the authors themselves don't know I exist.

If I'm feeling generous, or my shelf is looking a little empty, I may further blur the line between fiction and reality, shelving titles here because I feel they *could* be friends. I'm not talking about the author this time, but the characters themselves: Anne Shirley, Jo March, Veronica Mars . . . I could go on, but you're already questioning my judgment, I'm sure.

When I started my friends and family shelf, I felt a little silly; I had to be embarrassingly creative with my definition to fill it, in the beginning. Do my family members write books? (No.) Do I have enough writerly friends to fill a bookshelf? (No.)

Envy is a deadly sin, but *bookshelf* envy has proven to be a source of inspiration. Reorganizing my shelves has changed the way I think about books and the people who write them. Here on these shelves I've gathered my own inner circle: the books I feel closest to, the people who matter to me.

7

Life Imitates Art

People read for a multiplicity of reasons. Nearly forty years in, I can tell you why I inhale books like oxygen: I'm grateful for my one life, but I'd prefer to live a thousand—and my favorite books allow me to experience more on the page than I ever could in my actual life. A good book allows me to step into another world, to experience people and places and situations foreign to my own day-to-day existence. I love experiencing the new, the novel, the otherwise impossible—especially when I can do it from my own comfy chair.

Books have another advantage over reality. In books, we often encounter those things *first*, vicariously experiencing rites of passage on the page long before we live them for ourselves—we fall in love, or suffer a bad breakup; we lose a beloved pet, or a parent. We go to college, take on a new job, fight with a roommate, bicker with a spouse.

Books draw us deeply into the lives of others, showing us the world through someone else's eyes, page after page. They take us to new and exciting places while meeting us right where we are, whisking us away to walk by the Seine or through a Saharan desert or down a Manhattan sidewalk.

Books provide a safe space to encounter new and unfamiliar situations, to practice living in unfamiliar environments, to test-drive encounters with new people and new experiences. Through our reading, we learn how to process triumph and fear and loss and sadness, to deal with annoying siblings or friend drama or something much, much worse. And when we get to that point in our real life when it's happening to *us*, it's not so unfamiliar. We've been there before, in a book.

This ability to "preview" real-life experiences through books is one of the big perks readers enjoy. But I didn't always think so.

As a child, whenever I felt a little out of place in my own life, sometimes I wished I could exchange my reality for the world in the pages, which seemed a little more meaningful and a lot more interesting than my own ordinary experience. My middle-class, grade-school upbringing felt mundane compared to the lives I read about in fiction; I wanted to be Caddie Woodlawn or Sara Crewe or Alice through the looking glass. I didn't want my life to imitate art; I wanted what I read to remind me of something I had already experienced.

I am low-grade obsessed with the 1990s movie *You've Got Mail*, a 1990s *Pride and Prejudice*–inspired romantic comedy featuring Meg Ryan as indie bookseller Kathleen Kelly and Tom Hanks as her rival, Joe Fox, owner of the big bad box store Fox Books that threatens to put her out of business. It's got everything I love—Jane Austen, Manhattan's Upper West Side, a world of books and reading—so it's no surprise I've seen it an embarrassing number of times.

I was in college when I first saw *You've Got Mail*, and I loved Kathleen Kelly instantly. I was mostly past my wistful grade-school days of wishing myself into every novel I read, but I was alarmingly struck by how she echoed my old fear of settling for my real life, musing in one scene, "So much of what I see reminds me of something I read in a book, when shouldn't it be the other way around?"

Her impetus was this: once she'd read a story about a butterfly in a subway train, and then . . . she saw one! The film shows Kathleen rattling along on the train, an open book in her lap, when a butterfly suddenly flits into her field of vision. You can *see* her visceral delight. That thing she'd only read about had come true.

Yet she wondered if her experience was cheapened because she'd *read* it before she *lived* it, and my twenty-year-old self wondered right along with her. But I'm not the girl—or the reader—I was then, and I now know the times when reading cheapens *anything* are few and far between. I've seen how our on-the-page experiences set the stage for our actual lives. Our books frame the scenes for us so we can better understand and experience what's happening when it happens to *us*—whether that's transitioning to a new line of work, or grieving an unexpected loss, or vacationing in Tuscany.

Sometimes our on-the-page experiences mean so much to us that we create a real-life experience that *intentionally* imitates art. We sign up for a class or take on a project, travel to a different city, or, in our case, visit a certain bookstore. We show up to meet the authors who penned our favorite contemporary novels, or trek to the homes of the greats, maybe Austen or Brontë, Fitzgerald or Faulkner—visits significant not just because they happen in our "real life," but because they're rooted in what we first read.

I've been dragging my husband to literary destinations for years, but last year my whole family got in on the action, making a pilgrimage of sorts to Manhattan's Books of Wonder, one of the bookstores that inspired The Shop Around the Corner in *You've Got Mail*. My family loves to visit bookstores, and Books of Wonder is especially lovely. But what really made the experience for us was that we'd already encountered this store before—in fiction.

Many years after I saw *You've Got Mail* for the first time, I was on a train, high in the Colorado mountains. The day was sunny and warm, the windows were open, and as we climbed, a butterfly fluttered in through the open window across the aisle. It floated down the length of our car, paused a moment, and flitted out through another window, back into the mountain air.

That thing I'd first experienced so many years ago in fiction was happening to *me*—and my experience was richer for it. Because a story planted that idea in my imagination all those years ago, it meant something more when it happened to me, in my own life. It called back a special moment I had already experienced through art, and it didn't make it less meaningful.

With apologies to Kathleen Kelly, what I've come to learn is this: if my real life reminds me of something I read in a book, I'm reading well—and I'm probably living well, too.

8

How to Organize
Your Bookshelves

1. For beautifully styled bookshelves, follow this decorators' rule of thumb: each bookshelf should hold one-third books, one-third accessories, and one-third empty space.

2. You're a book lover; you don't have enough shelves to begin with. Ignore the decorators.

3. Determine a method of organization. Alphabetical order ensures you will be able to find any given title, but this is only the beginning of the avid reader's concerns. The Dewey Decimal System will wow your

friends and ensure they'll talk about you at cocktail parties. Organize by color, and everyone who doesn't organize their books by the rainbow will think your efforts are seriously misguided, but your shelves will be breathtaking. To relish the twin delights of baffling your friends and finding your books, organize by Trivial Pursuit category.

4. Stay open to possibility; you'll change your system soon enough. Some people play tennis in their spare time. Others knit or scrapbook. You're a reader; your hobby is organizing your bookshelves.

5. Develop strong feelings about dust jackets. Leave dust jackets in place and shelve your books, because dust jackets are an important part of the design process. Silently curse dust jackets every time you examine your bookshelves. Remove all dust jackets and place them in the recycling bin. Wait for regret to set in.

6. William Morris famously wrote, "Have nothing in your houses that you do not know to be useful, or believe to be beautiful." Make William Morris your guide. Buy books you don't like and will never read because they are beautiful: Reader's Digest Condensed Classics, classic Penguin editions of any genre, abridged editions of anything at all.

The lower the literary merit, the more attractive the book should be.

7. To "quiet" the room, arrange books with the spines facing in, like you saw on Pinterest. You won't be able to find anything you're looking for, but it will look nice.

8. Cull duplicates. If you have two copies of a book, keep the prettier one.

9. If you can't bring yourself to get rid of your duplicates, buy a third copy. When it comes to books, two is the loneliest number. Multiple copies of a single title are acceptable. Many, many multiples are preferable to two or three; excess makes you look interesting. Your friends may use the word *obsessed*, but they can't deny your obsession is interesting.

10. Start a collection. Signed copies or first editions are popular choices, but not the only ones. Find all the copies you can of your favorite novel—including reprints and foreign translations—or all the works of your favorite author. Collect by "list," gathering together all the winners of the Pulitzer Prize, or the Hugo Award, or Newbery. Accumulate all the copies you can on a topic of interest, be it cottage gardening or personality typing or the National Park System. Or purchase books of the same collection, because

they look well together on the shelf: sophisticated clothbound volumes or cheerful Harper Perennial Olive Edition paperbacks, colorful illustrated classics for children, or gorgeous leather-bound classics for grown-ups. Group your collection together on your shelf. If you organize by alphabetical order or color, this will destroy your system.

11. Reconsider your system. Consult #4.

12. Remove the titles you don't like from your shelves and drop them in the nearest Little Free Library. But if you have more shelves than books, keep them for now. Less-than-cherished books are better than no books.

13. If you have more books than shelves, consider that any shelf holding books is a bookshelf.

14. If you still have more books than shelves, build more bookshelves. Author Anna Quindlen, who is to be trusted on such matters, wrote, "I would be most content if my children grew up to be the kind of people who think decorating consists mostly of building enough bookshelves." We are readers. This is how we decorate.

9

Book Bossy

Once upon a time, a dear friend suffered a breakup—a horrible breakup that's certainly five times worse than whatever you're imagining. In the aftermath, I wanted to make her feel better. And reader, I did a terrible thing. Well-intentioned, but terrible. I sent her a book. Well, two books.

Of the first, I regret nothing. I'd stumbled upon a review online about a new book on a subject that fascinated and perplexed her; I was fairly certain she wouldn't know of this new book's existence, and I thought it was the right amount of quirky and strange so that even if the book proved to be forgettable, she would feel that I had not forgotten *her*. We're both longtime believers in bibliotherapy. Maybe it would distract her from her heartbreak for a time.

But the second book? Alas, I sent her a book I thought would be good for her, that she *should* read, that would make her a better person. A book that would be character-building. A book I didn't necessarily think she *would* like, but thought she *should* like. It was a statement about the kind of person I thought she should be, not the kind of person she was or wanted to be. If my first book communicated *I love you and I'm thinking about you*, the second one shouted, *But can you pull it together already?* Not that I saw it at the time, because I was too busy being an idiot.

I wanted what was best for my friend, and my book recommendation—if you can call it that—reflected that. But because of its subject matter, that book also reflected that I thought her life was a Big Fat Mess at the moment, and she should do something about it.

This was not my proudest moment. You shouldn't tell a friend how to live her life, unless she asks—and even if she does, proceed with caution. This I knew. But I didn't perceive that giving books is no different. You shouldn't tell another grown-up what to read, or when, or how. Unless they ask, even the best book recommendation— with everything it telegraphs about your opinion of the reader—can feel like the literary version of unsolicited advice: unwelcome, unwanted, unhelpful.

I'd been bossy. Book bossy.

When my family moved to a new zip code last year, we faced the daunting prospect of moving our entire book collection. We don't own as many as some people do, but moving books is no fun, and to move fewer of them, I returned many titles I'd borrowed. We pass books around our friend and family circles all the time; ours is a lending lifestyle. As I piled the stack of books to be returned in my entryway, I noticed they had something in common: *I hadn't read any of them.*

One title was about a specific social justice cause a friend wished I would join her in championing. Another was a novel she thought a devoted reader like me should have crossed off her list by now. One was about a hobby a friend thought might make me happier if I took it up. Another was about the benefits of daily meditation. They were books my friends wished I would read or thought I *should* be interested in.

Others I'd asked to borrow, even had made a special trip out to pick them up. In that case, *I* was the one wielding the insidious *s*-word, internally, thinking I should have read that title or author by now, or should be more knowledgeable about that specific subject.

Should is a dangerous word, a warning sign that we're crossing an important boundary and veering into book bossiness. *Should* is tangled up with guilt, frustration, and regret; we use it all the time, many of us to speak of the ways we wish we could be more, do more, or just be

different. Or that we wish our friends could be different, and they would if they knew what was good for them.

Should is bossy.

Not all book bossiness is equal: in the lower levels, "bossy" looks like bookish enthusiasm gone ever-so-slightly awry. Most of us don't set out to give orders to our fellow readers about their reading lives, but that's where we end up. This stage is characterized by unsolicited book recommendations, whether delivered in person, by text, or email, but always out of the clear blue.

Mid-level bossy territory: taking an unrequested book to a friend, dropping it in the mailbox, bringing it by their house, placing it in their hands over coffee. This stage may be escalated by any conversation involving the follow-up question, *Have you read that yet?*

Advanced book bossiness is characterized by specific and unsolicited troubleshooting of any aspect of a person's reading life. What books should they read to fill the woeful gaps in their education, or cure the glaring issues they're clearly having in their personal life? Which author's collection must they absolutely buy next because their home library can't be complete without it? How are they supposed to feel about a certain work? This stage may also be characterized by the strategic perusal of a reader's bookshelves, with commentary on what's worth reading and what isn't, and why, often accompanied by shakes of the head, gasps, sighs, tsks.

When I'm book bossy, I want to see myself as helpful, or knowledgeable, or loving, or smart. But what I'm doing is making judgments, delivering reading recommendations for books that will never be read, not because they weren't on point, but because of how they were delivered.

When I'm book bossy, nobody reads what I recommend— even if the book is a perfect match for a reader, even if she thinks her life will be better for reading it. And I don't blame her. I feel this way too. I suspect we all do. The harder I push a book on a reader, the less likely she is to read it. And nowhere is this truer than in my own home.

Take my kids, who love me, and do much of what I suggest—but not when I boss them about the reading life.

My kids are avid readers. They read regularly, and widely. I don't coach them on what to read, but they know they can ask me for recommendations. If I want one of my kids—or anybody else's kid—to read a book, however, the last thing I'm going to do is tell them, unsolicited, that they should read it. (And if I push too hard? Forget about it. They won't touch that book for *years*.)

But they will read just about anything—happily, and of their own initiative—if they think it's their own idea or their own decision. So I let them decide. I might mention to the school librarian that I think they'd love a certain title, or that a certain friend enjoyed it, but I will not tell my child he should read it unless he asks. And even then I won't use the bad *s*-word.

Readers want to discover what *they* want to read, and they want to discover it for themselves. Maybe imagine you're a girl devoted to *The Rules*—playing it coy, playing hard to get—who knows what she wants but isn't afraid to put you off to ultimately get it. *The Rules* may be full of suspect advice for your dating life, but it's proven to be a good strategy for the reading life.

10

Bookworm Problems

Your library holds all come in at the same time. You have reached your limit on library checkouts, but nine books are waiting for you on hold. You must decide which books to let go of to remain in the library's good graces.

You check out more library books than you can carry. You check out more library books than can fit in your tote bag. You forget your tote bag. You visit the library in rain that's coming down so hard your tote bag is powerless against it. You don't live next door to the library anymore, so you don't pick up your reserves every day. You don't pick up your reserves for a week, and your stack is enormous. You pile the stack in your passenger seat, and your car yells at you because it thinks you have an unbuckled passenger.

You take five books to the pool because you can't decide what to read next. You can't comfortably manage your purse because you shoved three books in on the way out the door, unable to decide what to read next. You pack twelve books for a five-day vacation because you can't decide what to read next.

You're in the middle of a great book, but you need to go to work. Or to dinner. Or to bed. You're in the middle of a great book, and you forget to eat dinner. You keep reading "just one more chapter" until 2:00 a.m., and you cannot keep your eyes open the next day.

Your favorite book becomes a movie, and you're terrified to see it because you're fond of the way you picture the characters and hear their voices in your head. They make your favorite book into a movie and delete your favorite scene. They make your favorite book into a movie and it's terrible.

You are one-third of the way into a good book, and you realize you accidentally purchased the abridged version. You realize halfway through a book that it's part of a series, and you inadvertently began with book four. You finish a book with a cliff-hanger ending, immediately look for the next book in the series, and realize the author hasn't even begun writing the next installment. The anticipated publication date is four years away.

After much anticipation, your favorite author's long-awaited new title finally comes out. It's terrible.

Airplane travel is required, yet the airline frowns on you lugging the crate full of books you typically stash in your trunk for road trips on board.

You realize halfway through a boring flight that your new ebook purchase didn't download. Your Kindle battery dies halfway through a long flight. Your Kindle battery dies right when you get to the good part.

A delivery truck falls over in the middle of Pennsylvania, and your books are on it. An ice storm incapacitates the shipping hub in Dallas, and your books are in it.

You finally persuade your friend to read your lifetime favorite book. She gives it three stars. You persuade your husband to read one of your favorites. He pronounces it "fine." You cannot, no matter how much you beg, plead, or wheedle, convince your book club to read your favorite book. You cannot, no matter how or what you try, persuade your child to read your favorite childhood book. You convince your child to read your favorite childhood book, and he begins, but then says, "I just can't get into it."

Your To Be Read list holds 8,972 titles, and you want to read every one. Your TBR list is unquestionably too long to finish before you die. Your TBR list is longer than your arm, but you still can't decide what to read next. You have countless unread books at home, yet you feel like you have nothing to read. You have countless unread books at home, but the only book you're in the mood to read won't be published for six more weeks. You have countless unread books at home, but you can't resist buying one more.

You don't know how to pronounce a character's name, and you can't truly know the character until you know for certain you're saying the name right. You want to tell the world about a great book you read, but you don't know how to pronounce the author's name. You want to tell the world about a book you loved, but you fear your friends won't be able to see past the terrible cover. You want to tell the world about a book you loved, but the title is stupid. You realize midsentence that you have no idea how to say a certain word *out loud*, because until now you've only said it to yourself, in your head, while reading.

You fall asleep reading, and you wake up hours later with a terrible crick in your neck. You're reading in a moving vehicle, and it's making you queasy. You consider switching to the audio version, but if you do, it will take you much longer to get to the ending. You keep reading.

You decide to buy a book, but the only edition available is the movie tie-in edition. You want to buy a friend a Drop Caps hardcover as a gift—one of those gorgeous, expensive classics with the monogram on the cover—but the one with their initial is a book you both hated, or the color is brown. Your bookstore is having a three-for-two sale. You easily find the first two, but you cannot for the life of you decide on a third book. You buy nothing. You regret it later.

You find yourself alarmingly invested in the lives of fictional characters. You refer to fictional favorites in conversation as though they're your friends, and your real friends don't know who you're talking about. Your explanation puzzles your friends. You know you refer to a favorite book irritatingly often, but you can't stop.

Someone asks you to name your three favorite books, and you can narrow your list to only five. Or seven. Or seventeen.

You can't put the book you just finished behind you because you still want to live it. You have a terrible book hangover, and it lasts three days. Ibuprofen does nothing for it. You're sad because whatever you read next can't possibly be as good as the book you just finished. You despair because nothing you read can possibly be as good, ever again.

You finish an amazing series and need to grieve that it's over. You need to mourn the loss of a beloved character. You wonder why these events have no cultural markers, because you definitely need one.

Your home is a disaster except for your bookshelves, which are immaculate. Your house is a disaster because books cover every surface. Your house is a disaster because a clean house is a sign of a misspent life, and you spend yours reading.

You're at a killer used book sale and can't remember if you already own a certain title. You decide you do and come home. You were wrong and regret your lost chance. You decide you don't and come home and shelve your newly purchased third copy. You accidentally buy two of the same book at the book sale.

You have more books than shoes. You have more books than bookshelves. You do some quick math and realize how much money is tied up in your book collection. You suspect your books equal the gross domestic product of a small nation.

You accept that it's time to cull your personal library. You lovingly handle each book, determining if it brings you joy. It does. They all do. You are full of bookish joy, but still woefully short on shelf space.

11

The Readers I Have Been

I feel certain of this: I wouldn't be the person I am today if I weren't a reader. I don't just mean because I enjoy reading or spend so much time with my books. I mean that from an early age, and without consciously intending to, the ideas I got from books formed the interior architecture of my mind. As I read, unbeknownst to me, my brain was busily constructing a framework from the ideas in the pages, a framework I would continue building on and refining for years to come. At this point in my life, I'm mostly moving the mental furniture around and hanging new art on the walls, but every so often I add a new room, or move a support beam; occasionally a load-bearing wall needs to be relocated. But I'm long past the point of starting from scratch; I can work only with what's already there.

I can't name every title or author whose words are bricks in my mental house; their words snuck in too long ago or under the radar of my consciousness. But some authors occupy such an outsized place in my mind—their words have been so formative—that I can almost point to the specific bricks their works put in place. One of these is Madeleine L'Engle, who first won me over when I was a kid meeting *A Wrinkle in Time*, and later when I was a young mother. I began reading her memoirs at the urging of a friend, and when I encountered her phrase "the tired thirties" to describe the decade between thirty and forty, during which she would often literally fall asleep with her head against the typewriter, I knew she could be trusted. L'Engle knew a thing or two about the stages of a woman's life, and she wrote frequently about the process of growing up and growing older.

L'Engle once wrote, "The great thing about getting older is you don't lose all the other ages you've been." She writes in *The Irrational Season*, "I am not an isolated fifty-seven years old; I am every other age I have been, one, two, three, four, five, six, seven . . . all the way up to and occasionally beyond my present chronology."

Every adult has arrived there by passing through their childhood, then teens and twentysomethings. But according to Madeleine—and I'm inclined to believe her—

not every person can access their inner child, teen, or twentysomething.

Surely you've had the experience of meeting someone and thinking, *It's impossible he was ever a child.* Is it wrong to hope I'll never be one of them? I'd like to think I can access my inner four-year-old—curious about the world, skeptical of her little brother, innocently kind, occasionally cruel, always trusting. My inner seven-year-old—full of imagination, turning the creek bed behind my house into a fantasy kingdom ruled by mice. My inner seventeen-year-old—falling in love for the first time, feeling very grown-up making decisions for her future, and at the same time, very young. And now, when I occasionally have moments when I glimpse what I might be like at forty-five, or sixty-eight, or ninety-two, or any of the years to come.

I'd like to add an addendum to Madeleine's theory. Just as I'm all the ages I have been, I'm all the *readers* I have been.

It's taken me decades to figure out what kind of reader I am, and "what *kind*" is probably inaccurate: I've been many kinds of readers over the years, and I remember them fondly. (Sometimes I think I can imagine the readers I might yet be.) I'm the sum of all these bookish memories. My head is so full of musings and insights and ideas from books that I'm not sure who I would be or how I would think if they were all taken away.

I'm still the three-year-old on my father's knee, begging him to read *The Story of the Apple* or *There's a Monster at the End of This Book* again and again. I'm still the eight-year-old who innocently filled her school reading sheet with over a hundred titles, unaware that the class average would be somewhere around thirty, and that this would bring her unwelcome special attention. (Thankfully, the pleasures of reading outweighed the discomfort.)

I'm still the cautious ten-year-old sitting in the fifth-grade classroom listening to her teacher read aloud, who witnessed *A Bridge to Terabithia* unravel a classroom of thirty-three kids, leaving half of us sobbing and the other half futilely attempting to hide our tears.

I'm still the eager tween who spent the firstfruits of her babysitting money on the newest installments of The Baby-Sitters Club series, and later, in the inevitable 1980s progression, the Sweet Valley High series, who thought a great book didn't cost more than four dollars and didn't take more than an afternoon to read. I'm still the thirteen-year-old middle schooler suffering through a run of competent but uninspiring Language Arts teachers, culminating in an in-depth study of the impenetrable *Song of Roland* in the spring of eighth grade.

I'm still the earnest high school student writing her first term papers and feeling pleasantly grown up, trekking to the big library downtown for research on a Saturday morning, pulling her first Harold Bloom off the shelves, leaving her contacts behind in favor of her glasses, because wasn't that what smart college girls did on the weekends? (I probably got *that* idea from a book.) I'm still the sixteen-year-old diving deep into *The Great Gatsby*, slightly put off by the strange title, surprising herself by not hating it, beginning to understand what a good writer could do with the written word and the depths of meaning hidden in plain sight behind billboards and lights and water.

I'm still the nineteen-year-old college freshman goggling over her first Annie Dillard, Eudora Welty, and Isabel Allende, and struggling through David Hume and Erik Erikson and Friedrich Nietzsche (in German!), who must have read for fun sometimes but can't remember what counted as fun back then. (I imagine paperbacks were involved.)

I'm still the twentysomething inhaling spiritual memoirs as though her life depends on it, and maybe it did—churning through Madeleine and Dallas and Underhill and Lewis and Kathleen Norris and Eugene Peterson and Barbara Brown Taylor like they are oxygen.

I'm still the twentysomething who doesn't know how to vet contemporary fiction, the new releases filling the bookstore shelves that haven't yet had the opportunity to stand the test of time, who somehow keeps finding her way to one modern lackluster title after another until—burned by too many disappointing modern works—she decides to reacquaint herself with the works that have endured: Jane Austen, *Jane Eyre*, *Anna Karenina*. (And thereby learning the timeless lesson that would serve me well in the years to come: if you're looking for a great book, going *old* is never a terrible idea.)

I'm still the young mother—twenty-five, twenty-six—reading *Frog and Toad* and *Little Bear* and *Five Little Monkeys* aloud on the couch to my firstborn, who, being too young to reliably hold up his own head, neither understands nor cares what I read him. But *The Read-Aloud Handbook* validates my desire to read to my tiny baby, so I do. I'm still the reader who knew *Machines at Work* and *Chicka Chicka Boom Boom* by heart, from repetition. (To this day, I can't stop myself from announcing mealtimes with, "Now, let's eat lunch," because I read those words so many times in Byron Barton's board book. I am still this reader, even at lunchtime.)

I'm still the thirty-year-old discovering the pleasures of returning over and over again to a good novel, the reader who learned that you don't have to be a kid to read kid lit, who revisited Anne and Emily and Valancy, who indulged in the pleasures of filling the inexplicable gaps in her book-filled childhood, remedying the situation by speeding through all the Little House books, then the Betsy-Tacy books, and the Shoe series. Who blazed through all the Harry Potters in ten days, because they were *that good*.

I'm still the thirty-five-year-old who has the house to herself and a zillion things to do and two hours to do it in, but spends the time in an uncomfortable kitchen chair, finishing *Eleanor & Park* because she has to find out what happens next, and because that discovery feels like enough of an accomplishment for one afternoon.

And what of the reader I am today, now, reading for my own sake, because I love it, because it fuels me, and reading for and with the people I love? Reading books with ridiculous potty jokes because they delight my young children; reading books riddled with teen drama because those stories captivate my older kids. Reading a new-to-me author, falling in love, and binge reading everything she's ever written in a week, just as I did when I was younger. Visiting the bookstore three times a week and perusing the "new fiction" table every time, even though the titles haven't changed a whit, because I notice something a little bit different every time, and because a bookstore is full of nothing if not possibility. Still finding it hard to give up on any book with a catchy premise and great narrative drive, because I am *still* hooked on the story.

As a devoted reader, I know what it means for books to shape you—the person you are, the person you were then.

For readers, the great thing about getting older is that you don't lose all the other readers you've been. Sometimes you think fondly of the readers you used to be; sometimes looking back makes you cringe a little. But they're still here. They're still *you*.

12

What I Need Is a Deadline

On a gorgeous spring day, I was walking into the library, carrying a gigantic stack of books to return, when I bumped into a friend shouldering an equally formidable stack she'd just checked out.

We laughed about our respective burdens, shifting our awkward loads from arm to arm, attempting to ease the encroaching ache. "We are ridiculous," my friend said. "But is it really our fault? In a perfect world, there would be no due dates."

No due dates. What book lover could argue with that? I laughed, and agreed, and then we hurried in our respective directions to unburden ourselves—my friend, to deposit her books into her car, and me, to dump mine at the circulation desk before picking up another armful of reserves and starting the cycle all over again.

As I came back out through those doors, weighed down by my fresh stack, I surveyed my library haul, feeling as accomplished as a long-ago hunter returning home with the makings of a feast and calculating how best to make use of my bounty. What was I reading now? What books sat on my nightstand at home? What new titles did I need to read, and when, to get through my stack before everything came due? I did my calculations, my friend's words still ringing in my ears.

No due dates. My, how that would change things. What would I do differently if the library wasn't waiting on me? A lot, actually. And now that I'm thinking about it, I'm not sure I'd like it. If I didn't *need* to get through my newly acquired stack before the due dates rolled around, would I read them as fast? Would I read them at all?

I doubt it.

Huh.

It seems I wouldn't read nearly as much, or as carefully, without my deadlines.

Like many avid readers, my shelves are overflowing (literally, more often than not) with books I want to read. In his excellent book *The Opposite of Spoiled*, Ron Lieber defines "rich" as having everything you need and most of what you want—the essentials, and a lot more besides.

He does not explain how insatiable book lust fits into this scheme, but it does appear that when it comes to books, I am wealthy—incredibly so.

My library holds an abundance of riches, and that's just the beginning of my stores. My local bookstore's shelves hold thousands of titles, and the clerks can track down almost anything I want. My friends would happily lend me books from their abundant collections. My own bookshelves could keep me happily busy for months, if not years: as of this moment, the shelves in my home library hold 114 books I want to read but haven't yet—and that's not counting the books scattered about the house, shelved in my office, stacked by my nightstand, hiding in my children's rooms. The limitations on my reading choices are few.

Oh, but the time! Admittedly, I'm a fast reader: my default speed tilts toward the higher end of the spectrum. And yet, even if I were to read one book every day, that's just 365 books a year—an impressive statistic in a conversation about reading habits, but a mere fraction of the titles published in just a week. Even if I lived to be a healthy eighty years old, that's still less than thirty thousand titles read in a lifetime—not a small number, but only a sliver of the titles published during that period. And what of all the books that came before?

Choosing my next book sometimes feels like a complicated dance. With so many books to read, how can I

possibly decide what to read? What to read now? What
to read *next*? There are many factors to juggle, but I'll
tell you this: I agree with Duke Ellington, the jazz great
who famously quipped, "I don't need time. What I need
is a deadline."

A deadline—apologies to my library patron friend—
isn't an obstacle to my reading life. (My fines might tell

a different story, but never mind those.) In the face of overwhelming options, a deadline clarifies what I want to read *right now*. It focuses my attention on what I want to happen next. Just like a journalist who lives and dies by their deadline, a *reading* deadline ensures my books get read sooner, not later.

I often tell myself I'll get around to reading a certain book *one day*. But good intentions are worth only so much, and sometimes *one day* never comes. A good deadline forces me to ask myself if I'm ready to read it *right now*. (If I'm not, does it even belong on my To Be Read list?)

As deadlines go, library due dates aren't particularly frightening, but they still impose a clarifying framework on my stack of books to be read—especially if the book in question is an in-demand title I've waited months for. The library will deliver those requested titles to me, free of charge, but not without a price. Once they arrive, no matter when they come in, I have only three weeks to read them. If I've been waiting months for a popular book, I need to read it immediately or lose my chance. Long-awaited library books often become "urgent" items on my reading list, jumping ahead of books free of time constraints.

Sometimes a social obligation keeps my reading on schedule. Book club is obvious—how many readers spend an entire month *not* reading, only to read two hundred pages in the twenty-four hours before book club? But coffee with a friend may be enough to get me to read a certain book, and fast. When I have a coffee date on my calendar, I want to show up having read the book a friend raved about the last time we saw each other, because I know she's going to ask me about it. Sometimes I feel a pleasant kind of obligation to finish a certain title as quickly as possible because a friend is itching to borrow my copy, especially if it's a new release. I believe in sharing the book love, and so I read—quickly.

Even on vacation, a good deadline spurs me to read more: if I don't finish at least half of the physical books I brought on vacation, I'll feel like a failure (and my husband will tease me mercilessly).

Lately, my kids inspire me to read more, *and* fast. When my child is reading a book and wants to talk about it *right now* . . . well, I want to talk about books with my kids, so I need to read it. Now. My daughter knows my taste in literature pretty well. She'll often finish a book and say, "Mom, you *have* to read this"—and press it into my hands. She'll then proceed to ask me daily if I've read that book yet, the one she adored and thinks I will too.

It hurts my children's feelings not to read what they want me to read, and so I do, on deadline. Duke Ellington understands: "Without a deadline, baby, I wouldn't do nothing." Without a deadline, Duke, I wouldn't do *nothing*—but I wouldn't read as much either. And, baby, I love to read.

13

Keep Reading

As a reader who will surely die with thousands of unread books on her To Be Read list, I'm not keen on reading extra words—those pages in the book that aren't part of the text. I tend to greet a critic's introduction to a new classic edition with skepticism, and even an author's note at the front of a reprint may not seem worth the ink. Perhaps that introduction is filler, and I can skip straight to chapter one. If it isn't strictly part of the narrative, I don't need to read it, right? For many, many years, I happily counted the author's acknowledgments as *extra*, skipping right over them, grateful that I could move on to the next book a little more quickly.

I wish I could pinpoint the exact moment I first decided to take time to read the author's extra notes at the end of the book. What book prompted me to keep turning its pages instead of moving straight to the next book? What did that author say? Who did they thank, and why did their words hook me? I wish I could remember what they said that charmed me—because *charm* they did. I'm still more likely than not to skip over a critic's introduction to the twentieth anniversary edition of a book, but I no longer skip the acknowledgments. And I don't just read them—I read them *first*, before I read anything else in the pages. And then, if they're good, I'll probably read them again. And again and again, just to myself, or out loud to whoever is around to listen.

That is, if they're good. The best acknowledgments are endearing and entertaining, witty and wise, short but not too short, sweet but not sappy. They're funny, or strange, or surprising. They're personal and positive. You can tell a lot about a person by who they choose to thank, and how, and for what; in the best acknowledgments, their gratitude spills off the page.

I may not want to spend my precious time reading extra words, but I'll always make time to read a few more pages of behind-the-scenes scoop—especially when it's coming straight from the author. Now that I've seen the light, I deeply regret not reading acknowledgments in books before, because so many times the authors' acknowledgments have deepened my appreciation for and understanding of the story.

In *A Deeper Darkness*, J. T. Ellison describes the friendly fire wartime incident that inspired the plot of her military mystery. In *A Great Reckoning*, Louise Penny speaks of her husband's dementia and the enormous kindness they've encountered since his diagnosis, as well as her gratitude for those whose help enabled her to go into her living room, open her laptop, and spend time in the company of her other friends—the characters in her book. In *Seabiscuit*, Laura Hillenbrand explains how writing her book had been "a four-year lesson in how history hides in curious places." She tells readers how after exhausting the expected sources for her research—newspaper archives, magazines, racing histories—she turned to the unconventional, going as far as placing "information wanted" ads and making calls to hundreds of strangers in her search for untold stories about her subjects.

In these pages, I've discovered who came up with a book's title or central idea or championed the inclusion of a certain chapter. In *In the Midst of Winter*, Isabel Allende explains that she didn't know what to write about, so certain friends brainstormed the ideas that became the book's skeleton. (She also reveals she always starts her books on January 8.) In *Station Eleven*, Emily St. John

Mandel acknowledges her debt of inspiration to the *Daily Mail* article that inspired the chapters of her book set in Malaysia. In *Love and First Sight*, a young adult novel my whole family loved, Josh Sundquist thanks his agent for playing matchmaker with two of his characters, giving his novel the love story it was missing.

Sometimes the acknowledgments hint at how the book in my hands almost *didn't* come to be, or at the improbable circumstances that led to its publication. In *The Things We Wish Were True*, Marybeth Whalen thanks her agent, who "called late one Tuesday night and told me not to give up, and then didn't give up, either." In *Four Seasons in Rome*, Anthony Doerr thanks the publishing professional "who convinced me my notebooks might be worth transforming into a book." In *Major Pettigrew's Last Stand*, Helen Simonson begins her acknowledgments with the origin story of her literary career: "A long time ago, a stay-at-home mother in Brooklyn, who missed her busy advertising job, stumbled into a writing class at New York's 92nd Street Y looking for a creative outlet."

From the acknowledgments we learn the details it was important the author get right: what it's like to live in a certain place or time or to hold a certain occupation, or what the finer points of a theory are. In *Empire Falls*, Richard Russo thanks his daughter Kate "for reminding me by means of concrete detail just how horrible high school can be, and how lucky we all are to escape more or less intact." In *A God in Ruins*, Kate Atkinson thanks the director of the Yorkshire Air Museum, "who answered my (probably annoying) questions so fully." In *Dark Matter*, Blake Crouch thanks the physics and astronomy professor who "helped me not to look like a total idiot in discussing the broad-stroke concepts of quantum mechanics."

In the acknowledgments, you see time and again who had their hands in the story, how it takes not just an author but a proverbial village to bring a book to life. (Julie Buxbaum kicks off her *What to Say Next* acknowledgments with a joke: if you didn't like her novel, here are all the other people you can blame.)

In *Lab Girl*, Hope Jahren thanks her agent for teaching her "the difference between a bunch of stories and a book." In *Salvage the Bones*, Jesmyn Ward thanks her agent, "who believed from the first word." In *Love Walked In*, Marisa de los Santos thanks her agent "for her immense sanity and patience." In *The Hate U Give*, Angie Thomas thanks *her* agent (or, more precisely, "superhero agent extraordinaire"), saying he's her biggest cheerleader and also her psychologist every now and then.

In *Empire Falls* (perhaps my favorite acknowledgments ever), Richard Russo thanks his editor, saying, "I'd attempt to describe my gratitude in words, but then he'd have to edit them, and he's worked too hard already." In *Ex Libris*,

Anne Fadiman thanks her editor, who edited her essays "with such meticulous expertise that I was sometimes tempted to junk my own words and publish his marginalia." In *A Million Little Ways*, Emily P. Freeman especially thanks her editor "for not accepting the first draft of this book." In *The Power of Habit*, Charles Duhigg thanks his editor, saying, "I'd heard from some friends that he had elevated their prose and held their hands so gracefully they almost forgot the touch. But I figured they were exaggerating, since many of them were drinking at the time. Dear reader: it's all true."

In their acknowledgments, authors shower praise on the oft-unsung behind-the-scenes crew. In *The Wife, the Maid, and the Mistress*, Ariel Lawhon credits her copy editor with "the patience of Job and the thoroughness of the IRS." In *Small Victories*, Anne Lamott thanks her longtime copy editor, saying, "You have saved me from looking illiterate more times than I can count." In *The Last Ballad*, Wiley Cash thanks his publicist, "who always finds the way." In *Gold*, Chris Cleave thanks his book's art director and designer, saying, "If you first picked up this book because it looked good, I owe them one."

I'm a reader who always wondered what the writing life was like, and not knowing the details, supplied my own—imagining writers cozied in garret apartments with old-fashioned typewriters and endless cups of tea. But in the acknowledgments, the authors hint at the practicalities of writing books, brass-tacks details that might otherwise never occur to readers. They may casually mention that they were three years behind on their deadline, or that they never could have met that deadline without the assistance of the freezer section at Trader Joe's. Or that their local Apple Store employee saved their presumed lost manuscript in their hour of need, or that their child's technological troubleshooting was invaluable.

In the acknowledgments, authors confess that they couldn't have written the book were it not for summer vacation, or the rhythms of the school year. Laura Vanderkam, now a mother of four, jokes in *I Know How She Does It*, "Someday I won't be asking editors to set deadlines around my due dates." In *Dreamland Burning*, Jennifer Latham thanks her kids "for putting up with Deadline Jen and I-Can't-Right-Now-I'm-Working Mom." Fredrik Backman closes *Beartown* with a final word to his children: "Thank you for waiting while I wrote this. NOW we can play *Minecraft*."

In the acknowledgments, authors also thank the people who don't make the writing happen, or make it better, but make it possible for the writing *to* happen. They thank the gym community that helped them stay sane while on deadline, or the singers whose soundtracks kept them company while they wrote. In *Daily Rituals*, Mason Currey thanks the friend "who helped me hang on to my day job and did me the great kindness of constantly asking how the book was coming along." In *Rules of Civility*, Manhattanite Amor Towles thanks "all the excellent purveyors of coffee from Canal Street to Union Square" (and also Bob Dylan, "for creating several lifetimes' worth of inspiration"). In *Short Trip to the Edge*, Scott Cairns thanks Jackson Browne, "whose songs during the seventies made me want to become a poet."* In *Falling Free*, Shannan Martin thanks her local shop The Electric Brew for "the hot Earl Grey, the white noise, the community, and the space." In *Lie to Me*, J. T. Ellison thanks her local joint Grays on Main for the people-watching, writing space, and beverages.

Authors thank their grade-school teachers, their college professors, their fellow students. They thank their favorite childhood bookstores, the librarians who shelved all the books they borrowed for reading and research, or the booksellers who hand-sell their titles to their customers. In *The Last Ballad*, Wiley Cash thanks "the librarians and booksellers who sustain the creative, intellectual, and civic life of our nation." In *The Almost Sisters*, Joshilyn Jackson thanks the "Righteous Handsellers, especially those of you who have pressed my books into the hands

---

*This is part of the dedication, not the acknowledgments, but the book doesn't have acknowledgments, and that Browne bit is too good to pass up.

of the right readers and said, 'You are going to love this.'"
In the acknowledgments, authors thank their readers, over
and over, for reading their work, thus making it possible
for them to live the writing life.

In *The Secret Life of Bees*, Sue Monk Kidd thanks her
parents, saying they're nothing like the oppressive parents
in her story. In *Drive*, Dan Pink tells his reader he's grateful for his wife, who "read every word I wrote—including
many thousands of them aloud while I sat in a red chair
cringing at their sound." (Though my favorite part is when
he thanks her "for these small reasons, and many larger
ones that are none of your business.") In *Peace Like a
River*, Leif Enger thanks his mother, "who read us Robert
Louis Stevenson before we could talk, and who writes
better letters than anyone since the Apostle Paul." In *The
Power of Habit*, Charles Duhigg thanks *his* parents, who
"encouraged me from a young age to write, even as I was
setting things on fire and giving them reason to figure that
future correspondence might be on prison stationery."

I especially enjoy stumbling across miscellaneous good-
ies and oddities, the things an author can't include anywhere else. In his acknowledgments for *The Read-Aloud
Handbook*, Jim Trelease thanks his neighbor, "whose enthusiasm for my idea spilled over at a family reunion ten
years ago within hearing distance of a fledgling literary
agent." In *A Piece of the World*, Christina Baker Kline

reveals two biographies were so crucial to her work that she called them her "touchstones," and that both became so tattered she needed to buy multiple copies.

In *What to Say Next*, Julie Buxbaum proclaims the greatest indie bookstore in the world is A Great Place for Good Books. In *The Things We Wish Were True*, Marybeth Whalen promises a friend she'll name a character for her in her next book. In a chapter of *But What If We're Wrong?* Chuck Klosterman tells a story about watching a hedgehog outside his window in Akron. But in his acknowledgments, he explains he's since discovered his memory can't be true because hedgehogs aren't native to North America. ("I have to assume this is not a well-known fact, since I've been telling this anecdote for almost two decades and not one person has ever remarked, 'Hey idiot, don't you realize there are no hedgehogs in Ohio?'") And I'm still trying to figure out this thanks from Tana French in *The Trespasser*: "David Ryan, top with smoked ham, bacon strips, ground beef, mushrooms, and black olives, bake for ten minutes on pizza stone, serve with German Pilsner."

Readers, a book may be long, but the acknowledgments are short—and the return on your reading time is enormous. Get yourself to the bookstore or library, or perhaps to your own bookshelves. Pull down some books, open them to the acknowledgments pages, and see what you've been missing.

14

A Reader's Coming of Age

It's a truism that early reading shapes the reader you become. We look back wistfully at the readers we were as children, and at the books we read on our parents' knees, the ones we read under the covers with our flashlights, the ones we giggled over with friends. Then there were the books we read in school, from kindergarten to high school and maybe beyond, under the guidance of other readers who hopefully illuminated the meaning of what we read.

But then it happens. School is over, classes are done, and we become responsible for our *own* reading lives. Nobody else is in charge of what we read; those decisions are now all ours. Now *we* choose what kind of readers we want to be; *we* choose which pages will fill our lives.

We don't enter adulthood as fully formed adults, nor do we enter adulthood as fully formed readers. When I graduated, I knew I still had a lot of growing up to do, but nobody told me I had to grow up as a reader too.

Every reader goes through this rite of passage: the transition from having books chosen *for* us to choosing books for ourselves. When given the choice, some choose *not* to read. But you, dear reader, moved from being told what to read to choosing for yourself. From reading on assignment, perhaps to please someone else, to reading at your own leisure to please only yourself. When faced with the task of establishing your own reading life, you did it, or maybe you're still in the middle of doing it.

Like other kinds of growing up, this doesn't happen overnight. The transition happens slowly, over time. We make a reading life by reading, and we stumble as we figure it out, learning through trial and error not just *what* to read for ourselves, but how. Establishing not just that we *will* be readers, but determining what *kind* of readers we will be.

Luckily, I didn't know all that as a young reader. In my early twenties, I was wholly occupied with establishing my new adult life: I graduated from college, started a new job, got married, and moved into my first house. That was enough adult pressure to deal with; I'm glad I didn't know then that over the next few years I would set the course for my reading life as well.

I didn't feel like a grown-up, because I was still growing up myself, but I couldn't articulate that then. Yet because I *was* still very much growing up, the books I chose for myself would both keep me company on the journey and influence the kind of person I'd ultimately grow up to be. Books are powerful like that.

And what to choose? This is where my story, perhaps like all stories about reading, is intimately tangled up with place. When it comes to our reading lives, place matters, whether metaphorical or literal. I was in a place of transition and in a physical place where good books were easy to come by. And so I read.

When I think about growing up as a reader, about coming into my own as one and claiming responsibility for my own reading life, the scenes that play out in my head are from this early era. Those formative years in my early to midtwenties left an indelible mark on the person and reader I would become. Those first years are when I laid the foundation I'm building on even now.

When you're not sure what you should read for the rest of your life, the library is a good place to start. So I went there, often, sampling widely. I can picture myself, strolling down the shady library path that ran right by our driveway, taking the long way on a beautiful day or the short direct route on a rainy or hot one, arms full to bursting with stacks of books. (So lavish that I was occasionally

98

embarrassed by how I was taxing the library's resources, although my librarians never complained; instead they congratulated me on my stacks and stacks.) We passed books around our circle of friends, rarely getting together without coming or going with a book in hand—loaning one out, or bringing a new-to-me borrowed title back home. Plus my husband and I each brought our own book collections to our marriage, childhood favorites and other titles we'd picked up along the way that remained unread. It was easy to experiment, to dabble—I was surrounded by good books.

Scientists say that when it comes to nostalgia, scent trumps all other senses because of its uncanny ability to tap straight into our emotional memories. Catch a whiff of caramelized apples, and you're suddenly five years old again, safe and warm in your mother's kitchen. The scent of magnolia reminds you of summer afternoons in your grandmother's living room, where she floated blossoms in crystal bowls on her coffee table. A hint of printer toner takes you back to sixteen, standing at the copy machine at your first job. The smell of Earl Grey and I'm eighteen, bent over my books while my British roommate prepares yet another cup for a late-night study session.

Book lovers have strong feelings about bookish scents; some of us get poetic about the distinctive smell of freshly inked paper, or old cloth-covered hardcovers, or a used bookstore. I've never cared for the smell of used bookstores myself, but as a devoted reader, I've noticed how the books themselves serve as portals to my past, conjuring similarly powerful memories. There's something about glimpsing, and especially handling, a book from long ago that takes me right back to where I was when I first read it. The book triggers memories of why I picked it up, how it made me feel, what was going on in my life at the time, transporting me so thoroughly that, for a moment, I feel like I'm there once again.

Even today, certain titles from my early twenties take me right back to my own coming of age as a reader.

Exhibit A: *Rebecca*, by Daphne du Maurier. Age twenty-two. Hardcover, large, black, crinkly polyester wrapper, 456 pages. Library. I'd never heard of it before a friend mentioned over dinner that she'd read it in two days because it was *that* good. When my library request came in, I was there waiting when the library opened (alas, not till 10:00 a.m.) to check it out. I sprawled across my bed and read four hundred pages in a single day. I didn't know a book could be that absorbing, especially not one written in 1938.

Exhibit B: Simon Winchester's *The Professor and the Madman*. Age twenty-two. Audiobook, square plastic case, six CDs in sleeves. Library. Will and I were rolling tile-blue paint over the old mint green in the kitchen; it was tedious work, and we needed entertainment. I'd read about it in a magazine, the library had only the audiobook in its collection, and Will was up for something new. We thoroughly enjoyed the truth-is-stranger-than-fiction tale, so much so that we wanted to keep painting to listen. I didn't know the fun of experiencing a book with another reader. I didn't know that was something you could *do* outside the classroom.

Exhibit C: David Keirsey's *Please Understand Me II*. Age twenty-two. Blue paperback, worn, 350 pages. Library. We'd taken personality tests in premarital counseling; I was intrigued and wanted to know more. Read over a span of cold winter evenings, on a yellow sofa, cup of tea in hand. This book would change my understanding of myself and my marriage, and it planted the seeds of an idea that would, seventeen years later, become my first book.

Exhibit D: *Jane Eyre*, Charlotte Brontë. Age twenty-four. Pink Penguin paperback, 434 pages, never opened. Aspirational purchase by my teenage self at a local indie store. I'd never read this book, despite owning it for years, because I hadn't yet learned that "classic" did not equal "boring." But it was a Sunday afternoon, the library was closed, and I couldn't decide what to read next. So I contemplated the contents of my living room bookshelf, spied the pink paperback, and resolved that the time had come to cross a classic I should have read in high school off my

To Be Read list. I started reading, tentatively, in the sunny bay window and thought, *Why didn't anybody tell me this book was actually good?*

Exhibit E: *The Girlfriends' Guide to Pregnancy*, Vicki Iovine. Age twenty-four. Red-and-white paperback, new but soon-to-be well-worn, 288 pages. Purchased in desperation at the local bookstore after being scared sleepless one too many times by the ominous *What to Expect When You're Expecting*, which expected me to hit every pregnancy milestone a full month before I actually did. I needed alternatives, and I found one in Iovine, who walked me through my pregnancy (all four of them), providing the reassurance that my experience was normal and that it wasn't time to freak out just yet. But in turning to that book time and again, I was digging grooves and laying habits characteristic of avid readers: turning to books— and actual, physical books at that—for the information I wanted and needed, poring over books about cleaning and cooking and parenting and pregnancy, practical things, things I didn't know how to do yet. Further evidence: the constant churn of reading-for-information books through our house on cooking, cleaning, gardening, DIY-ing, parenting, and anything else I needed to know.

Exhibit F: *David Copperfield*. Age twenty-four. Black Penguin paperback, 718 pages, torn, smelled like old books. Extra-dark, close-set type, the kind that leaves inky smudges on your fingertips. Library. *Jane Eyre* changed things. When I was a student, those old books held zero appeal, but now I experienced the freedom to read not out of duty, nor for a grade, but because I *wanted* to. And because they were *good*. I got acquainted with my library's wall of paperback classics (which provided a clear visual on just how many books I should have read in high school), pleasantly pliable paperbacks that were more likely than not to deliver a solid reading experience, and there was *never* a wait for them. The tables had turned from my childhood years, when I used to read with a flashlight under the covers. Now I'd put my own baby to bed and was terrified to creep out of the room, lest I wake him. But I didn't even mind because I had my flashlight and Dickens. I was shocked at how much I enjoyed it.

Exhibit G: *Drowning Ruth*, Christina Schwarz. Age twenty-five. Not-quite-right plastic-wrapped hardcover, 352 pages. Confession: an Oprah Book Club selection. Library. By now I loved to read classics, and I loved to read nonfiction for information, but I consistently picked disappointing contemporary novels. This book was greatly important to me, not because I loved it (I didn't), but because it represented my tentative foray into the world of contemporary fiction. I read it quickly, in my bedroom before I went to sleep, propped against my headboard with a cup of tea. Something about it helped me begin to form my own judgments, state my own opinions, discern my own taste. I waded back into that world, a world I would in later years feel much more at home in, and those seeds started with this book.

By my midtwenties, I'd made the transition, establishing myself as a reader, coming into my own as one, carving out a space for my own reading life. Today I'm not the reader—or the person—I was at twenty-five; so much has changed in the intervening years, as it should. But it's then that the foundation was laid, in my fledgling first years of adulthood, when I made my reading life my own.

15

Bookseller for a Day

My earliest career aspirations did not involve the reading life. When adults started asking the unavoidable question, "What do you want to be when you grow up?" I answered as any respectable third grader would: president, astronaut, firefighter, country music singer.

It didn't last.

By the time I reached high school, my favorite career fantasy involved hand-selling books at a charming independent bookstore by day and living in a book-filled, walk-up studio by night. I didn't devote a lot of time to imagining how exactly I'd fill my workaday hours—hey, I was fifteen, what did I know?—but in my mind I dwelt on the important moments: leaning on the counter, telling a customer about a favorite title. Standing by the tall shelf, pointing to exactly the right book for a reader—or the reader's granddaughter, or wife, or friend. Climbing the library ladder, plucking a rarely requested title off the highest shelf for the customer who asked for it by name. And, in quiet moments, settling in behind the counter, a cup of steaming tea beside me, nose in a book. And not just any book—a gorgeous, literary hardcover, its cover a rich hue suited to the sepia tones of my daydreams.

I've dreamed of working in a bookstore, or owning a bookstore, or at the very least, of spending enough dollars at a bookstore that its denizens cheer my arrival and greet me by name, since I was a kid. In my imagination my bookstore is a friendly yet irresistible destination, a temple to the written word, a community hub, a spot where readers gather around the common love of reading, discuss lofty literary and quotidian concerns, always find the books they're looking for—and the toilets clean themselves.

I was head over heels in love with my imaginary bookstore, and I'd long been dreaming of working in such a place *one day*. But then a bona fide bookstore-owning friend offered me a temporary—*very* temporary—gig in her shop for one day. I was worried that working in an actual bookstore would totally burst my illustrious, imaginary bubble. Spoiler alert: it did not. But it did change the way I imagined the bookstore of my dreams. It changed the way I see *all* bookstores.

I love bookstores because *I love books*. In a bookstore, books are the stars. This focus is reflected in some bookstore names, like Alexandria's Hooray for Books!, Brooklyn's Books Are Magic, and Manhattan's Books of Wonder. Books *are* wondrous, no doubt about it. But my stint as a bookseller showed me that in addition to those glorious books, *the bookstore itself* is an unappreciated wonder. I was awed by my behind-the-scenes glimpse of how much work, planning, organizing, logistics, luck, and magic it takes to bring those books to the readers in a bricks-and-mortar store. I adore a good bookstore, yet I vastly underestimated what it took to operate *that* particular wonder.

First, the books themselves: the selection varies by store, of course—and then it varies by day. Each individual book is lovingly put together over the course of years by its author, with help from agents, editors, copy editors, art designers, cover directors, photographers, publicists, marketers, sales professionals, and more. These books cover every topic imaginable. Some came out last Tuesday; some came out two hundred years ago, or two thousand. Every day new books arrive in the store; every day readers buy books and take them home.

But how do those books get there?

Logistics are not my love language, so this is where I start feeling woozy. Several times a year, your local booksellers think about what books they want to appear on their shelves six to nine months later. Some booksellers handpick every title—thousands of them, perhaps tens of thousands. They scan the bookish horizons for new titles that pique their interest and carefully curate their stock to reflect the preferences and personalities of the people who work there and the readers who shop there. They order from publishers and distributors and sometimes authors themselves, and then these shipments originate in different towns and are carried across the country by several different delivery mechanisms, through heat and wind and rain and the occasional natural disaster.

And that's just the books! My favorite bookstores stock not only hardcovers and paperbacks, but maps of places real and fictional; mugs with store logos or pictures of bookshelves; pens, because readers love pens; socks and tote bags that look like library cards; and little buttons with tiny pictures of Elizabeth Bennet. The bookseller first selected and then ordered everything (all from different places, of course), and then *these* disparate goods (all invoiced separately) originate in different towns and are carried across the country (and sometimes the world) to come together under one roof.

Once the goods arrive, they still have to find their way into the hands of the right readers. Sometimes these readers know what they're looking for: their next book club selection, a gift for a grandchild, the next book in a favorite series.

Sometimes readers know what they're looking for, but they need help finding it. During my bookselling day, I discovered that an important part of the job is solving customers' mysteries.

"I didn't catch the title, but I heard about it on NPR, and the author used to date Steve Jobs."

"I forget the title, but it was published last week, and it's by a woman."

"I forget the title, but it has the word *man* in it, and I think it's blue." (If my experience is anything resembling typical, booksellers spend an astonishing portion of their days trying to come up with forgotten titles.)

Sometimes a reader doesn't know what she wants to read next, and she comes to the bookstore seeking the answer. Booksellers have a unique perspective on who is reading what: they see it on their floors every day. They're equipped to handle reader questions.

"I just finished *A Gentleman in Moscow*. Can you recommend something similar?"

"I loved *The Kitchen House*, but I need a change of pace."

"My book club loved *Middlemarch* but hated *Wuthering Heights*. What should we read next?"

Bookstores, by their nature, share much in common. I know the common features I love to see, which I seek out at every store I visit: a prominent new release table for fiction and nonfiction, a healthy "staff picks" selection, a rack of clever greeting cards, a children's section stocked full of colorful titles at the eye level of a four-year-old. These relative similarities make it even more striking in how they diverge, depending on each store's specific owner, approach, city, and culture. A whole section devoted to local authors and interests and attractions. A robust pen display, or a broad selection of local pottery or chocolates or coffee. An eclectic mix of books and gifts and stuff that makes you feel that store couldn't be anywhere other than St. Louis or Santa Cruz or Stockholm. The markers that tell you where you are, that say *You are here*.

My day as a bookseller did destroy one of my romantic illusions: the booksellers aren't sitting behind the counter losing themselves in good books. They're focused on the hundreds of small tasks it takes to get the right book into your hands. But it turns out that, for booksellers, putting those books into the hands of the right customers is the best part of the job.

16

Book Twins

It took me thirty-five years to find my twin. The resemblance is undeniable: we share the same outlook, style, and sensibility. At first glance we might seem one and the same, practically interchangeable. But those who know us well can tell us apart, seeing our similarities, yes, but also our subtle differences.

We're not bound by blood or formal ties. We've never shared a last name or an address or even Thanksgiving dinner. Our twinness is confined to our reading lives: she's that remarkable reader whose taste bears an astonishing resemblance to my own. My reading life has been better since I found her, simply because she steers me to read more of what I enjoy and less of what I don't. I was

dismayed when I once read that more books are published on any given Tuesday than I could read in an entire year, and that's just one Tuesday—and one year.

From the vast array of titles, how am I to find the books *I* will love, the ones that will feel like they're meant for *me*? I won't claim that despair never creeps in, but two readers can cover more ground than one. My twin discovers books I might otherwise have missed, she enthusiastically recommends books she's read and knows I will love, she sacrifices herself by reading a promising-sounding book that proves to be forgettable, thus saving me the time.

I do the same for her, pointing out titles she should prioritize, and titles she can safely skip, because I read them first and can confidently say her finite reading time is better spent elsewhere. Despite initial appearances, we aren't identical, and we've learned to vet books not just for ourselves, but for each other. She's comfortable going a little darker; I'm comfortable with more stylized prose. She has more patience for the magical; I'll put up with the sappy. We know each other's tastes, and we each read more great books than we used to, because we've discovered a shortcut to finding the good stuff.

A book twin is a joy, and I highly recommend finding one, if you can. But as a reader, I'm up against centuries of must-read literature, with more pouring forth every week. It's great to have a twin, but I'm grateful for my wider literary family. If we're to divide and conquer these titles, we need each other. I'm constantly on the lookout for like-minded readers, those kindred spirits whose circles overlap my own on the Venn diagram of reading tastes. I would be lost without my fellow readers who tell me what they enjoyed, and why. Who give me clues as to what *I* will enjoy, or not. Will that book be worth my time? I rely on my reader companions to guide me. I know their taste, and I understand how it relates to my own.

Once, on the field hockey sidelines, I overheard one parent gushing to another about a book she had just finished. "It's the best book I've read all year!" she raved. "Do you like to read? You *have* to read it. I *know* you'll love it!"

Her enthusiasm attracted the attention of other parents nearby. "What book is this?" they asked. She shared the title, urging them all to read it immediately. "You will *all* love it," she assured them. "*Everyone* should read it."

I stole a glance over my shoulder. I didn't know the excited reader, but I could see other parents reaching for iPhones and notepads to take down the title; one woman announced she'd just bought it online, on the spot. I opened my mouth, and then shut it again. She wasn't talking to me. Deep breath. Another. Oh, *help*. What's a reader to do? Because I *hated* that book.

It was fresh on my mind; I'd read it just the week before. I'd opened it on a Saturday morning and quickly realized it probably wasn't right for me but kept reading. I'll say this for the book: it had narrative drive. I was curious about what would happen next—and I kept turning the pages, even though the story made me cringe, even though I suspected I'd regret the time spent on it. I finished the next day, and as I turned the last page, all I could think was, *Did I just choose to spend four hours of my life on* this?

I sat on the sidelines and ran through my options: Should I speak up for the common good? What were my obligations to my fellow readers? Was I blowing this out of proportion?

I decided the answer to the last question was definitely "maybe," and I kept my mouth shut. Besides, I didn't know their taste. It wasn't the right book for me, but it could have been right for those readers. But that conversation got me thinking: I rely heavily on my fellow readers to find great books to read. I spend my precious and finite reading time on the books I'm most excited about—and more often than not, my excitement springs from another reader's enthusiastic recommendation.

Bookish enthusiasm is contagious, but it isn't sufficient—not if I want to find the books that are truly right for me, and for you to find the ones right for you. It's easy enough for me to say, "I liked that book," or "I didn't," but I often struggle to explain why. I'm constantly surprised at how difficult it is to articulate my thoughts on what I've read in a way that is coherent, useful, and enjoyable, whether I'm sharing a five-thousand-word formal review or a twenty-word text message. But I feel I owe it to my fellow readers to try, because my comments help others decide what is worth reading and what should be read next.

I dread the feeling of closing a book, thinking, *Did I just choose to spend four hours of my life on* this? I'm certain it will happen again; it's a peril of the reading life. But in recent years, two things have helped me keep that sinking feeling at bay.

The first is how I choose my books: I've always striven to be a careful reader, one who thoughtfully engages with what she's reading; I've learned to bring that same level of care not just to reading, but to choosing which books to read in the first place.

The second is my book twin, who, knowing my taste, throws good books in my path and steers me away from the duds. You can have a vibrant reading life without one, I suppose. But I'm glad I don't have to.

17

Again, for the First Time

My parents moved into their current home when I was two years old. One advantage to their not moving while my brother and I were growing up (or since) was this: upstairs in the corner bathroom—the one that was mine—is an old strip of paint on one side of the door frame. My parents have taken good care of their home, but this door frame hasn't been painted since shortly after they moved in.

That's because once my brother and I were able to stand on our own, my mom measured us against that door frame every so often, recording our current height with her pencil, marking our growth. As we were growing up, we could look at both the current and past markings to see how much we'd changed.

Like so many readers, I maintain a virtual shelf on Goodreads of books I'd like to read one day. I haven't added to this shelf in *years*; it isn't how I track my pressing, highest priority reads. Despite my neglect, this shelf holds 819 titles I would very much like to read one day.

I'm far from alone with my massive To Be Read list—on Goodreads and elsewhere—and I doubt my number even counts as "massive" by some readers' standards. Despite this list, which will surely not only remain unfinished when I die, but grow ever longer until then, I am an avid *re*reader of good books.

Many devoted readers, lovers of good literature, never read the same book twice. Their TBR list is too long to justify spending time on books they've already read, they say. I'm sympathetic to their point of view. But I'm not about to change my rereading ways. I've found that a good book not only holds up to repeated visits, but improves each time we return to it.

Thousands of years ago, the Greek philosopher Heraclitus wrote, "No man ever steps in the same river twice, for it's not the same river and he's not the same man." That growth chart in my parents' house isn't being updated anymore; I'm long past the stage of growing three inches a year. But *I* am still growing, changing—not the kind of growth you can measure against a door frame, but the kind you can see measured against the books I've read. Books worth coming back to, not just because they keep changing for me, but because *I* am changing as well.

When I find myself in a dreaded reading slump, nothing boosts me out of it faster than revisiting an old favorite. Old books, like old friends, are good for the soul. But they're not just comfort reads. No, a good book is *exciting* to return to, because even though I've been there before, the landscape is always changing. I notice something new each time I read a great book. As Italo Calvino wrote, "A classic is a book that has never finished saying what it has to say." Great books keep surprising me with new things.

Sometimes this has to do with my point of view, with what I know when I open the book. The first time I read a book, I immerse myself in the story. I'm not concerned with catching every nuance; if it's truly a good book, I couldn't do that even if I wanted to. The first time, I want to find out *what happens*. Who are these people in the pages, what do they want, why do they matter? On my first pass, I'm figuring it all out. On the second pass, the experience is qualitatively different. Read *Anne of Green Gables* once, and you're shocked when she cracks the slate over Gilbert's head. Read it the second time, and you read that scene through the lens of knowing everything that will come after. Read *Persuasion* the first time, and you shudder at every successive relational plot turn. Read it again, and—remembering the ending—you read it differently, knowing every character's inner thoughts, motivations, and shortly-to-follow resolutions.

I experienced this vividly recently when I reread *Crossing to Safety* for the fourth or fifth time. Stegner's work continues to improve for me on each successive reading. (It took me four or five times through before I finally grasped the meaning of the title.) The book opens with unfamiliar characters, approaching what is soon to become a

deathbed. The first time I read the book I was confused: I didn't know these people, or why they were gathered, or how they'd ended up here, or what they were feeling. The second time, when I already knew the intricacies of the plot, I was caught off guard by my immediate tears. I had been unprepared for the difference, but there it was: this time I *knew* these people, and I stepped immediately into their sorrow. It was the difference between glimpsing a stranger's funeral procession from afar and participating in a loved one's, up close.

That book wasn't quite the same when I read it again, but not just because of what I knew about the book. No, the book was different because *I* was different. Since the last time I read the book, my own reality had changed.

In *Crossing to Safety*, Stegner lays out the stories of two ordinary couples and their intertwined lives, using their relationships to explore themes that matter to me— love and friendship, work and marriage, suffering and loss. Larry is a writer, underwhelmed by his own success; Sally contracts a sudden and incurable illness and faces it bravely; Sid is a man in love, whose beloved wife pushes him around; Charity's shadow falls over all—she's a dominant personality who orchestrates everyone else's lives. These characters feel like friends to me, and while some may raise an eyebrow at that sentiment, devoted readers know what I mean.

Rereading can make you remember who you used to be, and, like pencil marks on a door frame, show you how much you've changed. The first time I read *Crossing to Safety*, I was younger. When I reread it recently, I had more experiences to draw on as I read, having done some growing up in the interim. I knew more of friendship and love, of loss and suffering. When we revisit a book we've read before, we see how life has woken us up to understand passages that previously went over our heads. The book itself highlights the gap between who I am and who I used to be. I imagine this is why readers frequently revisit their childhood favorites: they take us back to who we were then, reminding us of times long gone by. Rereading helps us see how *we* have changed. (For this reason, I should probably be required to reread everything I read as a teenager.) The experience is immensely different, for better or worse.

And it *can* be worse. Some readers claim they avoid rereading out of fear: What if a book they loved back then disappoints them now? They're afraid a favorite won't be as good as they remember—and they would be devastated if the book didn't live up to their own fond memories. Perhaps it's better not to risk it.

This happens to me, of course. Sometimes books are not as good as I remember—or rather, I don't enjoy them as much as I remembered, not because my earlier judgment was wrong, but because *I* have changed. This happened to me with *Pilgrim at Tinker Creek*, an excellent book that blew me away when I first read it. The first time through I found it revolutionary. The second time, though worthwhile, didn't live up to my own expectations—but how could it have? When I first encountered *Pilgrim* as a college freshman, I had never read anything quite like it before. My first experience was made great by the thrill of discovery. On my second read, I experienced no such thrill, because I already knew the work. This is as it should be, and yet it hurts to see what we've lost. Sometimes that loss looks like change.

Heraclitus also wrote, "A man's character is his fate." A reader's character is *her* fate—and I'm determined to remain open to new experiences in the same old (new) books, to see the ways I've changed and how those books have too.

A good book, when we return to it, will always have something new to say. It's not the same book, and we're not the same reader.

18

Book People

Like many couples, my parents had differing opinions when it came to their stuff. My mom was fond of regularly "emancipating" her possessions (which is a fancy way of saying the folks at Goodwill's donation drop-off window saw her often enough to greet her by name). My dad was more of a collector, and the difference was obvious in their respective book collections. The bulk of my mom's holdings filled a single kitchen shelf; my father needed whole rooms to contain his.

I was particularly fascinated by the density and sheer volume of books in my father's study. There were books on shallow open shelves and books stacked high against the wall. A large wardrobe—wide and deep like the Narnia variety—held hundreds more titles, and *these* books were shelved three layers deep: books behind books behind books. On lazy afternoons I'd settle myself, cross-legged on the floor, in front of the wardrobe to explore what exactly was in there. My method involved pulling armfuls of books from the first layer to expose the second, setting neat stacks all around me until I hit the wardrobe's back wall. I felt like I was digging for buried treasure, and looking back, I don't think my first impression was too far off.

My mom caught me once, perched in front of that wardrobe, snooping in the very back for something good to read. I wasn't yet old enough to articulate the difference in my parents' collections, and for the first time it occurred to me to ask my mom where the rest of *her* books were. She paused and then said (rather carefully, I thought), "Your father grew up visiting the bookstore. I grew up visiting the library. We haven't really changed."

I am happy to report that, thanks to nature, nurture, and my parents' dissimilar habits, I grew up visiting both the library *and* the bookstore, and I haven't changed much either. My mom took me to the former, of course, giving me space to wander, browse the shelves at leisure, and check out whatever I wanted on my own library card. My father took me to the bookstore to do much of the same, except I had to buy any books I wanted to take home. A reader himself, he wanted to do his own browsing, and he encouraged me to do my own.

Before I grasped what habits were or why they mattered, my grooves had been dug deep: I'd become the kind of person who sought out books. The library served its purpose well, but given the choice as a kid, I'd take the bookstore every time.

My childhood bookstore was big, in that peculiar way common to bookstores of the 1990s. It wasn't delightfully cramped or cozy, as so many independent bookstores are now; I would never describe it as *intimate* or *charming*. No, this bookstore was *expansive*, squatting on the kind of square footage reserved today for sporting equipment or home goods or groceries. The atmosphere wasn't the big draw—I remember high ceilings, pale green walls, and yellow fluorescent lighting—but what it lacked in ambience, it made up for in books. That store was *packed* with books and people who loved them. They came to browse towering, well-stocked shelves and settle into enormous comfy chairs to read for hours, undisturbed.

My dad took me to that bookstore on quiet evenings and on busy weekends and every time in between. He would often pile my brother and me into the car and take us to the bookstore in moments when—I now recognize in hindsight—he wanted to give my mom a break. We'd browse on quiet Saturday afternoons when there was nothing much to do; we'd stop in while we were out running errands on busy days. Long wait at the area restaurant? No problem. We'd pass the hour at the bookstore. We'd visit in pursuit of a specific book—the next in a beloved series, a required read for school, a book recommended by a friend or teacher, perhaps one we'd heard about on the radio or seen in a magazine.

That store was a place where you could find what you were looking for. The expectation then, in the days before the internet, was if a reader wanted a book, it would be there, on the shelves. Sometimes we'd head to the bookstore when we wanted to find *something* to read but didn't yet know what it was. My purchases were small, but frequent—some planned, some serendipitous. I picked up inexpensive paperback classics, birthday presents, crossword puzzle books, SAT study guides. I went through a Nancy Drew phase, and then a Winnie the Pooh phase (in my teens!). One summer I developed a full-fledged picture book obsession and spent many a hot summer afternoon opening half the books in the children's section, ignoring the words, looking for beautiful pages to frame for my bedroom walls. I came home with books about quantum physics and dream interpretation and journaling. I spent a large percentage of my disposable income feeding my newly acquired stationery habit, firmly enabled by the bookstore's gorgeous offerings, saving my babysitting dollars to spend on decidedly frivolous packs of Crane letter sheets and Kate Spade note cards.

Once, as a fourteen-year-old, I chose *The Prince of Tides* from one of many staff picks shelves. I opened it that night, closed it forty pages later, properly traumatized, and took it back to the store the next week, determined to *give* it back if the store wouldn't issue me a refund. (They did.) As a fifteen-year-old, I bought a pink paperback *Jane Eyre* I wouldn't read for another ten years, though I didn't know it at the time. As a nineteen-year-old I took a chance on a new author, buying myself the first Harry Potter in hardcover and my cousin the audio version to keep her company on the cross-country road trip she would take back to college.

As I got older, visiting the bookstore seemed like a perfectly reasonable thing to do, even if my dad wasn't doing the driving. I'd head there with friends, or on a date, or to spend a pleasant hour by myself. I daydreamed of working there, and I idolized a friend's mother, who actually did. I confessed this to my friend, who tried to talk me out of it. "It has cachet, but it pays like McDonald's," she said of her mother's job. I was undeterred. Rumor had it that applicants had to pass a terribly difficult test, demonstrating their knowledge of books and reading, and I was newly starstruck by the staff—the book lovers who stocked the shelves, made recommendations, and took my money. They'd passed the test.

One summer, home from college for a few months, I submitted my application and, in a remote corner holding Latin American literature, faced the legendary test. It *was* hard. Until that moment, I didn't know how much I didn't know, both as a person and as a reader. (I was awfully cocky for a nineteen-year-old.) Six weeks later, long after I'd given up on my summer bookstore dreams and taken a babysitting job, the manager called and offered me the job. "I have to go back to school," I regretfully told her, but I relished the offer. That store never employed me, but it gave me bragging rights for years. I'm *still* bragging about it, often enough that were I to start the story again right now, my kids would ask, "This again?"

My kids know how I feel about the bookstore, and about the library. Rarely does a week go by that we don't pop in, together, to one or the other. When we're on the road, we seek out good books and new-to-us bookstores in the cities and towns we visit. We've bent our driving routes so we could visit not-quite-on-the-way bookstores, and we've even planned entire trips *because* we wanted to visit a certain bookstore. It's what we do. It's who we are.

I have hopes and dreams for my kids, as parents do. I hope they'll live right and live well, find love and fulfilling work, and not endure too much heartbreak on the way. And I also, specifically, hope that one day—when they're old enough to choose for themselves, apart from me—they'll discover that they too are book people. One day, not as far off as I would like, they'll head to the bookstore with friends, or on a date, or on a quiet weekend afternoon to spend a pleasant hour by themselves. Not out of habit or duty, but because reading is part of who they are. It's in their blood. They're book people.

19

Take Me Back

Sometimes I fantasize about getting my hands on my library records. I can log on to my computer right now, of course, to see my current checkouts, pending reserve requests, overdue books, and late fee balance—but that's not what I'm talking about. No, my recurring bookworm dream is to peruse my personal library history like it's a historical document.

My bookshelves show me the books I've bought or been given; I need only look at them to see, at a glance, what I've read. But my library books come into my house and go out again, leaving behind only memories and a jotted line in a journal (if I'm lucky). I long for a list that captures these ephemeral reads—all the books I've borrowed in a lifetime of reading, from last week's armful spanning back to when I was a seven-year-old kid with my first library card. I don't need many details—just the titles and dates would be fine—but oh, how I'd love to see them.

These records preserve what my memory has not. I remember the highlights of my grade-school checkouts, but much is lost to time. How I'd love to see the complete list of what I chose to read in second grade, or sixth, or tenth. I frequented the library regularly in high school, and I expect my checkout history would trigger many a memory of Saturday expeditions to the big branch downtown, in search of scholarly commentary on Fitzgerald, Hawthorne, Dostoyevsky—the subjects of my first tentative term papers. But when I chose my own leisure reading, what *was* I reading? I remember little, but I trust my records would bring it flooding back.

And what of the milestones in my life? I imagine my records would reveal my early, haphazard career exploration, and my impending, exotic first trips to London and Paris and Prague, and that time we moved into a house with a neglected formal garden I aspired to resurrect. Based on my borrowed titles alone, I'd be able to clearly see the months and years I spent away from my hometown, the one I'm happy to live in even now. I would be able to spot the summer I got engaged, when I checked out every book on wedding planning in the library system. The

month I learned I was pregnant and immediately cleared the shelves of *those* books. The sudden surge of board book checkouts a year later, after we'd added another tiny reader to our household. It's all right there, in my library records.

A few years ago my family moved from that house next door to the library to one a full mile away. (Gasp!) After a move, it takes a while to get the hang of new rhythms and new routes home. It took me even longer to get the hang of my new library routine. An auditor evaluating my library records would notice the change immediately: the steady trickle of fines I'd garnered over the years turned into an avalanche overnight; my steady stream of checkouts and returns became a weekly gorging and purging.

And what of my expanding interests, both personal and readerly? I expect I could pinpoint the library books that ignited my fascination with urban planning, or time management, or homesteading. My records must reveal the year I discovered Kate Morton, or Wendell Berry, or Wallace Stegner, and my subsequent binges of each author's work, in turn. I could definitely determine how many times I checked out the Harry Potter series, and *Anne of Green Gables*, and how many successive times I checked out *A Pattern Language* before I realized I should buy my own copy.

My photographer friend says a good photo album preserves two kinds of histories: the chronological and the emotional. The reminder of both what happened and what it meant to you. As a lifelong reader and library patron, I yearn for my own sort of album—one composed not of photographs, but of book titles and checkout dates. My simple rows of library records may not be as pretty as personal photographs, but when it comes to *remembering*— well, they take me right back.

20

Windows to the Soul

Not long ago, I sat down to coffee with a newish friend, one I didn't yet know terribly well. I hadn't taken my first sip when she said, "I know you're a reader. I want to read more, and I need some ideas. Tell me your favorite novel. Or a book that's changed your life. Anything."

I love talking books with friends and strangers alike, but as I opened my mouth to answer, I realized that she'd just asked an extremely personal question.

Aside from the sheer impossibility of choosing *just one* favorite book, her question was daunting for another reason: I felt like I'd been asked to lay my soul on the table. Reading is personal and never more so than when we're sharing why we connect with certain books.

In Gabrielle Zevin's delightful novel *The Storied Life of A. J. Fikry*, her fictional character owns a bookstore on a remote East Coast island. It's a love letter to the power of books and bookstores to bring people together. At one point, A. J. Fikry, a wise man despite his fictional status, explains to his daughter, "You know everything you need to know about a person from the answer to the question, *What is your favorite book?*"

I wasn't sure I was ready for this new friend to know everything about me.

I could have told her one of my favorites is Evelyn Waugh's *Brideshead Revisited*. I've read it half a dozen times; it's the only work of Waugh's I've enjoyed, and I've read them all. I love its sad tone, its haunting complexity, its poetry and metaphor, and I love that it doesn't end happily. What would these things say about me? Perhaps, if my friend hadn't read it, she'd think my choice meant I was the kind of person who was hung up on some stodgy old classic.

I could have told her I adore Wallace Stegner's *Crossing to Safety*, for its wistful story and gorgeous prose and Stegner's ability to conjure a moving tale out of the mundane events of ordinary life. My new friend might have branded me a hopeless romantic, an armchair philosopher, or maybe just a snob who reads only serious fiction.

Since my friend wanted book recommendations, I could have told her some of my more recent favorites. I loved Diana Gabaldon's *Outlander*; maybe she'd think I was the kind of person who enjoyed a good story, well told, and that I wasn't afraid of a six-hundred-page novel. Or maybe she'd think I was one of those women hung up on the steamy scenes featuring eighteenth-century Scottish warriors, or a romantic soul hooked on the idea of star-crossed lovers.

I could have recommended a fun, lighthearted, easy-reading novel, like Marisa de los Santos's *Love Walked In*. It's a practically perfect romantic comedy, even if it's probably not a book that will change your life. Maybe my friend would have thought *I* was fun, lighthearted, and easygoing, just like my favorite book. Or maybe she would have judged me to be a lightweight reader who only reads beachy reads.

I could have told her about Anne Fadiman's wonderful essay collection *Ex Libris: Confessions of a Common Reader*, in which she explores the pain and pleasure of merging libraries with a new spouse, confesses to utilizing questionable bookmark strategies, and self-identifies as a compulsive proofreader. When I called these essays smart, interesting, and laugh-out-loud funny, would my new friend have thought me a hopeless nerd? (Probably, but she wouldn't have been wrong.)

Reading is often viewed as a solitary act; that's one of the reasons I love it, and it's certainly my favorite escape and introvert coping strategy of choice. But reading is also a *social* act: readers love to connect over good books. If I read a book that legitimately changes my life (what a find!), or a book that becomes a new favorite, or even a breezy novel that's tons of fun, I can't wait to talk about it with my fellow readers.

So when my friend asked for a favorite book, I answered cautiously—but how could I help but answer?

Nothing ventured, nothing gained—and I've found talking about books to be a reliable shortcut to getting to the good stuff with our fellow readers, to cutting to the heart of what matters. That makes it a little dangerous, a little risky. When we share our favorite titles, we can't help but share ourselves as well. Shakespeare said the eyes are the windows to the soul, but we readers know one's bookshelves reveal just as much.

21

I'd Rather Be Reading

Have you had the experience of browsing through a good photo album? Maybe it was one with photos of you as a kid, or from a trip you took to Paris or Prague or Pittsburgh. You didn't remember that restaurant, or that haircut, or that sunset over the river, or those sunglasses that made your two-year-old look like a mini movie star—but when you see the photo, it all comes flooding back.

When I go on vacation, I prefer to live in the moment instead of recording the moment. Taking photos to memorialize the experience isn't as fun as actually experiencing it. But I feel like taking those photos is a gift to my future self. They'll let me continue to remember and enjoy the moment months, years, even decades from now.

That's how I feel about my reading journal. Show me a cover of any book I've read, and it will take me right back to where I was when I read it. Books are portals to all kinds of memories—but only if I can remember that I read them. Ask me the best books I've read this year and a half-dozen titles might spring to mind—but no more. If I can't see it, I can't remember it: off the top of my head, I'd be lucky to recall a quarter of what I've read. Last month is hard enough, but last year, or five or ten years ago? My memory lets me down. But paging through my book journal brings it all roaring back.

I would rather be reading than memorializing what I'm reading; I'd rather experience the thing than record the thing. But I've grudgingly learned to do it anyway, inspired, I'm sorry to say, by pure envy.

A friend has been diligently tracking every book she's read for the past twenty-plus years, since she was a kid. Her book journal is in a cheap spiral notebook—nothing special to look at—but when I first learned of it, I was inordinately (or maybe entirely appropriately) flooded with envy.

Some readers meticulously record the dates they read each title and where they were when they read it. They note favorite quotes, memorable scenes, and key insights. My friend's log was just a list of titles and the dates she read them, but the quantity of data—the sheer number of books read over more than two decades—served as a travelogue for her reading life. I didn't have my own, but I wanted one, badly enough that I began.

Mine is nothing special, just a simple log noting what I read, and when, with a little star to mark my favorites. It's not fancy, but it's mine.

Since my conversion, I've become excessively interested in how other readers document their reading life. Some keep simple logs like mine. Some assign star ratings or grades or percentage scores. Some log pages and pages of character studies and quotes to remember and the ideas that made them stop and think.

Some readers are loyal to certain websites, or apps, or social media platforms—a Goodreads list, a Pinterest board, a personalized Instagram hashtag. Some couldn't live without a thick-papered journal and a fountain pen, or their trusty spreadsheets, easily searched and sorted. One friend keeps a line-a-day journal, the five-year kind more typically used for traditional memory keeping, to record her book memories. They necessarily remind her of all her other memories, because, like many readers, that's how her brain functions. Another takes a photograph of every book she reads and binds those photos into scrapbooks, creating her own book of books, suitable for the coffee table. (*Want.*)

Every reader's journal is its own sort of amazing. What reader wouldn't want their own? And yet I sometimes find myself relapsing, not recording my books for a week or two, when my preference for living in the moment wins out over my desire to document for my future self. When this happens, a quick review of the benefits of journaling—the reasons I do it, the rewards that come if I do—provides the kick in the pants I need to pull out my journal and pen again, reigniting my zeal of the convert.

It's embarrassing to admit, but without logging what I read, I forget all about it. I retain the ideas, and remember them when they're triggered, but without referring to my journal, I can barely remember what I've been reading.

With my personal log, however, the title alone can serve the same purpose as that photo in the vacation scrapbook. My journal doesn't hold a pretty photo to admire, but my brain is eager to fill in the book's details. It conjures a mental image of where I was when I read it, where I got it, and—most of the time—why I picked it up in the first place, as well as what I thought about it. Did I like it or not, and how did it make me feel? All this from one line of a reading log.

Interestingly, I've noticed that when I record what I read, I'm not an impartial documenter. When I started logging my books, I was surprised to discover that the very act of documenting my reading life changes what I choose to read. "You get what you measure," a wise friend once told me. The act of tracking something changes the way we think about it. My reading log turned into an unexpected vehicle for self-discovery.

I believe in reading at whim, and I generally choose books that I'm in the mood for, trusting that my reading life will balance out in the end, that I'll rack up a nice variety of books read without too much conscious effort.

But with the clear data about my reading life in hand, I could see what my reading habits were truly like. Sometimes they disappointed me. I may have had a feeling I was veering in a certain direction, but there's nothing like seeing it confirmed on the page. With the actual data before me, I could no longer fool myself that I was reading more than I really was, or reading a wide variety of genres or plenty of diverse books when I wasn't. On the page, I might notice a lack of perceived substance, or an excess of fluff, or a bunch of dead white males, or a string of underwhelming titles. I couldn't argue with my reading log, and seeing the truth of my reading life inspires me to change it.

Logging my books changed my reading life in another way. The act of *writing things down* inspires me to read more. Sure, it's fun to add another completed title to my list. But my log also helps me notice when I'm in a busy period and reading takes a backseat, nudging me to do something about it before too many days go by without adding a book to my list.

Remembering what I've read doesn't just help *me*; my log also helps me give better book recommendations to other readers. When a friend asks for a solid book recommendation and nothing springs to mind, or I'm heading off to book club to discuss my loves and hates with fellow readers, or I'm gearing up for a literary matchmaking session with a friend or stranger, I always begin by flipping through my book journal.

Reader, if you'd rather live in your reading moment than document it, I totally get it. I'd rather be reading too. But learn from my bookish regret: I don't care what system you use (and I use the word *system* loosely) as long as you use one. Start today, because as soon as you begin, you're going to wish you'd begun sooner. Record your books as a gift to your future self, a travelogue you'll be able to pull off the shelf years from now, to remember the journey.

We are readers. Books grace our shelves and fill our homes with beauty; they dwell in our minds and occupy our thoughts. Books prompt us to spend pleasant hours alone and connect us with fellow readers. They invite us to escape into their pages for an afternoon, and they inspire us to reimagine our lives. Good reading journals provide glimpses of how we've spent our days, and they tell the story of our lives.

Acknowledgments

In a book about the reading life, it might seem silly to thank blog readers and podcast listeners, but endless thanks to the communities that have gathered around *Modern Mrs Darcy* and *What Should I Read Next?* We know the value of making books part of our lives. Thanks for being part of mine, and for inspiring this collection. *Ah, how good it is . . .*

To Holland Saltsman, for answering all my bookstore questions (and we both know how many there were), for commiserating when I'm in a reading slump, for freely sharing the amazing books you've been reading lately, and for graciously hosting me at your store—the fabulous The Novel Neighbor in Webster Groves, St. Louis—so I could live out my dreams of being a bookseller for a day. When young readers dream of growing up and one day becoming booksellers themselves, it's because they experienced the wonders of a store like yours.

To indie bookstore owners extraordinaire Annie Jones (The Bookshelf, Thomasville, Georgia), Andrea Griffith (Browsers Books, Olympia, Washington), and Adah Fitzgerald (Main Street Books, Davidson, North Carolina)—thanks for carrying the bookseller torch, for answering all my nosy questions, for showing me the heart of indie bookselling, and for your all-around, overflowing enthusiasm for books and bookselling. I'm fortunate to know you, and I fervently wish you could be *my* local booksellers.

Annie Spence, Joshilyn Jackson, Kathleen Grissom, Sarah Mackenzie, Jane Mount, and Ariel Lawhon graciously read early copies and provided words of endorsement for this collection. I can't thank you enough for your kindness and generosity, and I'm so happy the love of books and reading (and writing!) brought us together.

To the wonderful staff of the St. Matthews Eline Library in Louisville, Kentucky. We're lucky you were ours all those years. We miss you.

To my agent, Bill Jensen, for getting this idea from the beginning.

To my editor, Rebekah Guzman, for assuring me this collection was better than I thought, and then for making it much better than it was, and for talking me down a time or two in between.

Thanks to Dave Lewis, for casting the vision; Wendy Wetzel, for making things happen and making it look easy; art director Patti Brinks, for exquisite taste and solid judgment, and for turning my books into things of beauty; Brianna DeWitt, for smartly spreading the word; and the whole team at Baker. It's been a pleasure.

To my parents, who made sure I never wanted for books, among other things. Mom, thanks for taking me to the library all those years. Dad, thanks for taking me to the bookstore countless times, of course, and for all the happy reading memories. *A man in a striped suit was walking past a fruit store . . .*

To Ginger Horton, thanks for being my first reader. To Katie Earley, for tending to Pemberley so I could write. To Melissa Klassen, for your friendship, and for helping me pull it all together (or, let's be honest, for pulling it together *for* me).

To Will, for everything, and specifically this time for helping me find the thread.

To Jackson, Sarah, Lucy, and Silas, for being such delightful humans, and readers besides, and for putting up with me when I try to play it cool about your reading lives and utterly fail. I love you, and I think you're great. On to the next.

Works Referenced

Allen, Sarah Addison. *The Sugar Queen*. New York: Bantam, 2008.

Atkinson, Kate. *A God in Ruins*. New York: Little, Brown and Company, 2015.

Austen, Jane. *Pride and Prejudice*. New York: Penguin Classics, 2003.

Backman, Fredrik. *Beartown*. Translated by Neil Smith. New York: Atria, 2016.

Cairns, Scott. *Short Trip to the Edge*. New York: HarperCollins, 2007.

Calvino, Italo. *The Uses of Literature*. San Diego: Harcourt Brace, 1986.

Cash, Wiley. *The Last Ballad*. New York: William Morrow, 2017.

Cleave, Chris. *Gold*. New York: Simon and Schuster, 2012.

Crouch, Blake. *Dark Matter*. New York: Crown, 2016.

Currey, Mason. *Daily Rituals*. New York: Alfred A. Knopf, 2016.

De Los Santos, Marisa. *Love Walked In*. New York: Plume, 2005.

Doerr, Anthony. *Four Seasons in Rome: On Twins, Insomnia, and the Biggest Funeral in the History of the World*. New York: Scribner, 2007.

Duhigg, Charles. *The Power of Habit: Why We Do What We Do in Life and Business*. New York: Random House, 2012.

Enger, Leif. *Peace Like a River*. New York: Grove Press, 2001.

Freeman, Emily P. *A Million Little Ways: Uncover the Art You Were Made to Live*. Grand Rapids: Revell, 2013.

French, Tana. *The Trespasser*. New York: Viking, 2016.

Hillenbrand, Laura. *Seabiscuit: An American Legend*. New York: Ballantine, 2001.

Jackson, Joshilyn. *The Almost Sisters*. New York: William Morrow, 2017.

Jahren, Hope. *Lab Girl*. New York: Alfred A. Knopf, 2016.

Klosterman, Chuck. *But What If We're Wrong?: Thinking about the Present As If It Were the Past*. New York: Blue Rider Press, 2016.

Lamott, Anne. *Small Victories: Spotting Improbable Moments of Grace*. New York: Riverhead, 2014.

Latham, Jennifer. *Dreamland Burning*. New York: Little, Brown and Company, 2017.

Lawhon, Ariel. *The Wife, the Maid, and the Mistress*. New York: Anchor, 2014.

L'Engle, Madeleine. *The Irrational Season*. New York: Harper-Collins, 1977.

Lewis, C. S. *The Four Loves*. New York: Harcourt Brace, 1960.

Works Referenced

Martin, George R. R. *A Dance with Dragons*. New York: Bantam, 2011.

Martin, Shannan. *Falling Free: Rescued from the Life I Always Wanted*. Nashville: Thomas Nelson, 2016.

Morris, William. *On Art and Socialism*. New York: Dover Publications, 1999.

Pink, Daniel. *Drive: The Surprising Truth about What Motivates Us*. New York: Riverhead, 2009.

Quindlen, Anna. *Thinking Out Loud: On the Personal, the Political, the Public, and the Private*. New York: Ballantine, 1994.

Russo, Richard. *Empire Falls*. New York: Vintage Books, 2002.

Simonson, Helen. *Major Pettigrew's Last Stand*. New York: Random House, 2011.

Towles, Amor. *Rules of Civility*. New York: Penguin, 2011.

Trelease, Jim. *The Read-Aloud Handbook*. New York: Penguin, 1982.

Vanderkam, Laura. *I Know How She Does It: How Successful Women Make the Most of Their Time*. New York: Portfolio, 2015.

Ward, Jesmyn. *Salvage the Bones*. New York: Bloomsbury, 2011.

Whalen, Marybeth. *The Things We Wish Were True*. Seattle: Lake Union Publishing, 2016.

Zevin, Gabrielle. *The Storied Life of A. J. Fikry*. Chapel Hill: Algonquin, 2014.

153

About the Author

When it comes to approaching her writing and life, Anne Bogel takes a line from Emily Dickinson: "I dwell in possibility." She is adept at viewing old ideas from a fresh perspective and presenting them to the reader in such a way that they experience them as if for the first time.

In 2011, Anne launched her blog *Modern Mrs Darcy*, which derives its name from a Jane Austen book. It didn't slot neatly into the existing blog niches (although she's been pleased to hear it described as "a lifestyle blog for nerds"), yet it quickly gained a cult following of smart, thoughtful readers who love Anne's modus operandi of approaching old, familiar ideas from new and fresh angles.

Anne's readers like to read. While *Modern Mrs Darcy* isn't strictly a book blog, Anne writes frequently about books and reading. Her book lists are among her most popular posts. She is well known by readers, authors, and publishers as a tastemaker. In 2016, she launched her podcast *What Should I Read Next?*—a popular show devoted to literary matchmaking, bibliotherapy, and all things books and reading.

Anne lives in Louisville, Kentucky, with her husband and four children.

MODERN Mrs Darcy

Hi! I'm Anne

Connect with my blog, book club, and
podcast (*What Should I Read Next?*) at
ModernMrsDarcy.com and **AnneBogel.com**.

WHAT SHOULD I READ NEXT?

with anne bogel

 AnneBogel   AnneBogel   ModernMrsDarcy

Discover the Power of
Personality Literacy

"This is the book I didn't even know I was waiting for.
I can't wait to share it with everyone I know."

—**Emily P. Freeman**, *Wall Street Journal*
bestselling author of *Simply Tuesday*